# WARRIOR NOTES HOMESCHOOLING

**Science**
**Project Based**
**Learning**
2nd Grade
Units 4-6

# Warrior Notes Homeschooling

# Second Grade Science Project-Based Learning

## 1 John 4:19 TPT
"Our love for others is our grateful response to the love God first demonstrated to us."

## 1 Corinthians 13:2 TPT
"And if I were to have the gift of prophecy with a profound understanding of God's hidden secrets, and if I possessed unending supernatural knowledge, and if I had the greatest gift of faith that could move mountains, but have never learned to love, then I am nothing."

## Table of Contents

## Introduction

What is Project-Based Learning?
- -Driving question
- -Critical thinking and research
- -Collaboration
- -Communication
- -Technology integration

## Using this course

The parent/guardian and child will spend four weeks on each unit using the experiments and research to complete a project each week and make a final presentation at the end of the fourth week.

## Course Objectives

The child/children will learn about the human body, health and manners, and safety. Through studying these concepts, we connect the natural world to the spiritual world.

## Notes for the parent/teacher

Each unit will be a month-long PBL study. The parent can decide whether to spend five days on each week's project or complete everything in one day for that week.

## Scope and Sequence

## Unit 4: The Human Body

> Week 1: Hearing and Speaking
> Week 2: Bones and Muscles
> Week 3: Teeth, Heart and Lungs
> Week 4: The Human Body Unit Presentation

## Unit 5: Health and Manners

> Week 1: Habits, Nutrition
> Week 2: Cleanliness
> Week 3: Respect, Courtesy, Kindness, Thankfulness, Thoughtfulness
> Week 4: Health and Manners Unit Presentation

## Unit 6: Safety

> Week 1: At Home- Kitchen, Bathroom, Stairs, Gun Safety, Fire Safety
> Week 2: Away from Home: Police Officers and Parents
> Week 3: Bicycle Safety and Car Safety
> Week 4: Safety Unit Presentation

# Unit 4:
# The Human Body

# Week 1: Hearing and Speaking

When God created man, He gave him amazing organs and systems that are all connected. Humans live healthy lives when all the body parts are working together the way God designed.

**Ephesians 4:16** NKJV "from whom the whole body, joined and knit together by what every joint supplies, according to the effective working by which every part does its share, causes growth of the body for the edifying of itself in love."

The ear and voice box are two body parts that allow us to hear and speak. They both work using vibrations, which are called **sound waves**.

## What are the parts of the ear?

The ear is made up of 3 parts:
The **outer ear** is what you can see. The **earlobe** is the rounded part at the bottom of the outer ear. Next is the **ear canal** which has earwax in it. The **earwax** is sticky and catches any dirt so it doesn't get into the middle or inner ear. The ear canal is shaped like a small pipe. It collects sounds and sends them to the **eardrum** at the end of the canal. The eardrum is a very thin and delicate membrane that vibrates from the sounds.

The **middle ear** takes all the sounds from the eardrum and sends it through 3 small vibrating bones that are connected. These bones carry the vibrations all the way through to the inner ear. They are the **hammer**, **anvil**, and **stirrup**.

The **inner ear** has a coiled tube that looks like a snail. This is called the **cochlea** and it is full of thousands of receptor cells. These cells receive the vibrations from the stirrup and send messages about them through different nerves to the brain. The brain translates all of these messages and determines what the sounds are. This entire process takes less than a second.

## Why do we have two ears?

The brain needs 2 sets of messages from different locations to figure out where every sound is coming from. There is also liquid in our **semicircular canals** which help us to balance. This liquid is on both sides of our head equally so we have perfect balance.

## Do animals with bigger ears have better hearing?

The size of ears does not help with hearing. An elephant has extremely large ears, but they cannot hear as many sounds as a spider, dog, cat, whale, or human. A human ear depends on the cells inside their cochlea to hear well, not on the size of their outer ears.

## How do we measure sounds?

We use **decibels** to measure sound waves. The more decibels, the louder the sound. A whisper measures 10 decibels and a normal speaking voice is around 50 decibels. An explosion can measure 140 decibels.

## Why do some humans lose their hearing?

We can have permanent damage to our hearing cells in the cochlea if we regularly listen to sounds over 90 decibels, for a long time. This can be the sound of a plane taking off, loud music in headphones, a concert, or an explosion. The best way to keep our hearing cells safe and healthy in the inner ear is to wear ear protection and avoid listening to very loud music through headphones.

**Romans 10:17** NKJV "So then faith comes by hearing, and hearing by the word of God."

## What are the parts of the voice box?

The voice box is also called the **larynx** and it is located in the throat. It is made up of 3 parts:

The **epiglottis** is a flap of cartilage that covers over the windpipe when you are eating. Food needs to stay in the digestive system and not enter into the lungs and make it hard to breathe. The epiglottis is located at the top of the voice box behind the tongue. It moves when a person is talking. This is why it is difficult to breathe and speak and eat all at the same time.

Under the epiglottis are 2 strong strips of tissue and muscle called **vocal cords.** They open and close during breathing. When they are closed, air pushing through them causes the cords to vibrate and create sound waves. The volume and variety of these sound waves are changed by moving the lips and tongue changing your breathing.

**Cartilage** is the last part of the voice box and it keeps the vocal cords in place and moving properly. When this cartilage is damaged, it affects the vocal cords and the ability to speak. Some things that can damage the cartilage is screaming, talking too much, not drinking enough water, and smoking.

**Isaiah 55:11** NKJV "So shall My word be that goes forth from My mouth; it shall not return to Me void, but it shall accomplish what I please, and it shall prosper in the thing for which I sent it."

We have two projects for your child to choose from. Pick one to complete for the final presentation in this unit, or do both according to your time and resources.

# Project 1: Parts of the Ear

# Project 2: Sound Wave Experiments

# Parts of the Ear

The ear is made up of tiny parts that are all attached to each other. Sounds enter the outer ear and move through the outer, middle, and inner ear as vibrations called sound waves. Earwax in the outer ear is continuously made by skin cells and extremely helpful in keeping the middle and inner ears safe from dirt and infections.

The middle ear contains the hammer, anvil, and stirrup. They are so tiny that if you put all 3 of them together, they would be smaller than a dime. They are the smallest bones in the entire human body.

The inner ear has a cochlea that has special sensitive nerve endings in it that collect all the vibrations and send them in messages to the brain. The brain takes this information and uses it with the rest of the body.

The nerve endings in the cochlea are like delicate hairs and they can be damaged and even break off due to a very loud noise. If they break off, they do not grow back.

## Materials Needed:

- Parts of the Ear page
- construction paper
- scissors
- pencil
- color pencils
- thin markers
- glue stick and glue

# Directions:

**First**, read all of the descriptions for the parts of the ear below.

## Outer Ear
Ear lobe: The outermost part of the ear.
Ear canal: A small pipe that collects sound.
Eardrum: Thin, delicate membrane.

## Middle Ear
Hammer: The first of a small chain of 3 bones.
Anvil: The second of a small chain of 3 bones.
Stirrup: The third of a small chain of 3 bones.

## Inner Ear
Cochlea: The coiled tube that looks like a shell.
Semicircular canals: Three interconnected tubes that control balance.

**Second**, cut out the Parts of the Ear page and write in the name of each part.

**Third**, color the outer parts of the ear shades of yellow and brown. The middle parts of the ear shades of pink and red. The inner parts of the ear shades of blue and purple.

**Fourth**, take the glue stick and spread a lot of glue onto the ear canal. Put enough on so you can see the white, sticky substance. This is ear wax.

**Next**, draw little hairs onto the inside of the cochlea to show the nerve endings.

**Finally**, glue the completed Parts of the Ear page to a piece of construction paper.

Save your Parts of the Ear work for your final presentation at the end of this Human Body Unit.

# Parts of the Ear

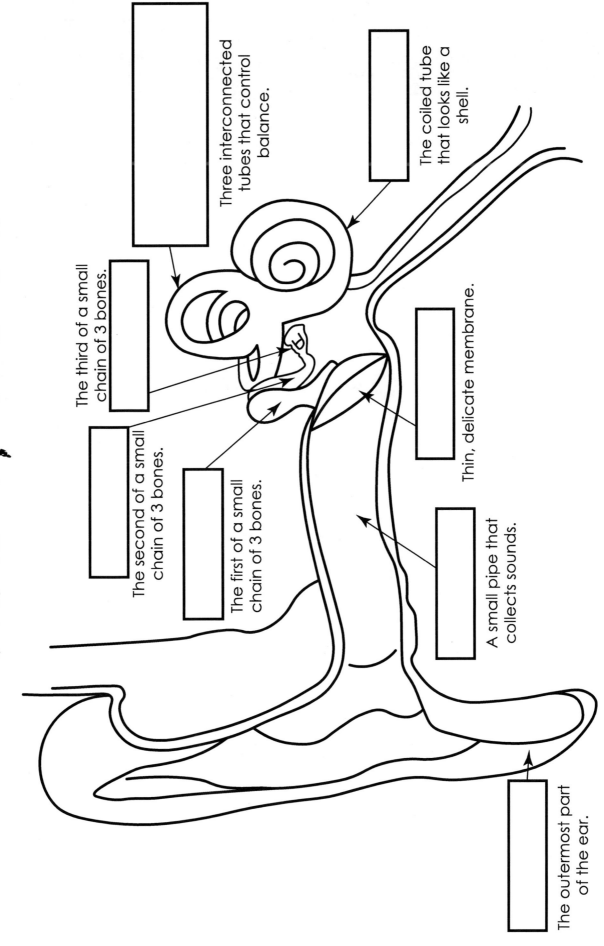

Three interconnected tubes that control balance.

The coiled tube that looks like a shell.

The third of a small chain of 3 bones.

The second of a small chain of 3 bones.

The first of a small chain of 3 bones.

Thin, delicate membrane.

A small pipe that collects sounds.

The outermost part of the ear.

# Sound Wave Experiments

Sound waves travel very fast, although not as fast as light waves. Our ears have to process through the sounds that move around us at an average of 800 miles per hour. Sound waves attach to the air, water, or other objects and this makes them change speed and direction.

**Revelation 14:2** NKJV "And I heard a voice from heaven, like the voice of many waters, and like the voice of loud thunder. And I heard the sound of harpists playing their harps."

Here are 6 different fun activities to complete that involve the sound waves we hear and the sound waves we speak. Choose at least 1 activity to try, and fill out the Sound Wave Experiment page to show what you learned.

## Spoon and Wall

## Materials Needed:

- Metal spoon
- Strand of thick string or yarn, 30 inches long

## Directions:

**First**, tie the spoon handle to the center of the string. Have a parent tie one end of the string to your pointer finger on one hand, and the other end of the string to your pointer finger on your other hand.

**Second**, put your pointer fingers into each outer ear so that you can't hear any sounds.

**Next**, lean over next to a wall so the spoon is hanging down in front of you. Now gently swing so the spoon hits the wall. You should hear the vibrations come through the string and into your ears.

Now swing it again but a little faster and stronger. You should hear a different sound come through the string into your ears.

Use this information to fill out the Sound Wave Experiment page.

# Sounds in the Water

## Materials needed:

- 1 Large disposable water bottle
- Plastic bucket
- Sharp scissors
- 2 Forks or spoons

## Directions:

**First**, fill the bucket about 3/4 full with water.

**Second**, have a parent cut off the very bottom of the disposable water bottle. Take off the lid and hold the bottom half of the water bottle in the water. Lean over and put your ear against the top of the bottle.

**Third**, have a parent hold the two forks or spoons under the water and bang them together several times. They will not hear anything, but you should be able to hear them loud and clear. Try banging them together softly and more strongly. Does the sound change?

Use this information to fill out the Sound Waves Experiment page.

# See the Sound

## Materials Needed:

- 1 Teaspoon of sugar
- Plastic wrap
- Large drinking glass
- Phone
- Rubber band

## Directions:

**First**, play a song on the phone loudly. Put the phone in the glass and put the plastic wrap over the top of the glass.

**Second**, wrap the plastic down with a rubber band so it is tightly on top of the glass.

**Third**, put the sugar on the top and middle of the plastic. Watch the sugar start to move as the sound waves vibrate the plastic wrap.

Now try it again with music on a different volume.

Use this information to fill out the Sound Wave Experiment page.

# Cup Messages

## Materials Needed:

- 2 Paper cups
- 50 Feet of string
- Scissors
- 2 Paper clips

## Directions:

**First**, have a parent use the scissors to poke a hole into the bottom of each cup.

**Second**, put each end of the string into the bottom hole of each cup and tie a knot in a paper clip to keep it from pulling back out through the hole.

**Third**, find someone to hold one cup and take the other cup and stand far away from each other so the string is tight. Make sure the string is not touching any objects.

**Now**, one at a time, speak into the cup while the other person puts their cup against their ear. Try this at different volumes and see if you can hear what they are saying. The sound waves will travel along the string and you can repeat back the message to the sender.

Use this information to fill out the Sound Wave Experiment page.

# Balloon Sounds

## Materials Needed:

Balloon

## Directions:

**First**, blow up the balloon until it is almost full and tie a knot in the end.

**Second**, hold it with both hands in front of your face and say "aaaaahh" in a medium voice. Notice how the balloon vibrates from the sound waves. Try this again using different volumes.

Now try holding the balloon in front of a radio or TV. Notice how the balloon vibrates differently.

Use this information to fill out the Sound Wave Experiment page.

# Sound Wave Experiment

What experiment or activity did you choose?

_____

Before trying the activity, what did you think would happen?

_____

What happened when you followed the directions?

_____

_____

_____

Did you try the activity more than once and change anything?
What happened the second time?

_____

What did you learn about sound waves from this activity?

_____

## Week 2: Bones and Muscles

**Ezekiel 37:5-6** NKJV "Thus says the Lord God to these bones: 'Surely I will cause breath to enter into you, and you shall live. I will put sinews on you and bring flesh upon you, cover you with skin and put breath in you; and you shall live. Then you shall know that I am the Lord.'"

God created the skeletal system when He created man so he would have a foundation to hold all of the other body parts and organs. The skeletal system is made up of 5 parts.

The largest part of the skeletal system is the bones. There are 206 **bones** in total. Bones are made of collagen and calcium. The area of the body with the most bones is in the wrists, hands, and fingers, which have 54 bones. The longest bone is the femur, which is the thigh bone. The strongest bones in the body are the hardest to break, and they are the femur and the skull. Bones protect your organs, like the heart and lungs, and they keep the shape of the body. You can keep your bones healthy by eating well and getting enough vitamins and especially calcium.

## Some bone names are:

humerus - upper arm

cranium - skull

femur - thigh

patella - kneecap

vertebrae - backbone

phalanges - fingers and toes

**Muscles** are sections and pieces of tissue that can contract and move to make force. They are attached to the bones and their main job is to move the bones. There are over 650 muscles in the whole body, and they are made of 79% water. The strongest muscle is the jaw. The muscle that works the most is the heart muscle. It never stops working, even when you're asleep, to move blood around your body.

Muscles are either **voluntary** or **involuntary**.

Involuntary muscles are automatic and you don't have to think about using them. One example is the muscles you use for breathing.

Voluntary muscles are the ones you can control, like the bicep muscle in your arm. Your brain makes your muscles move. The left side of your brain controls the muscles on the right side of your body and the right side of your brain controls the muscles on the left side of your body. You can control how healthy your muscles are by making sure to move them a lot with exercise.

## Some muscles names are:

bicep - front of the upper arm
tricep - back of the upper arm
quadriceps - front of thigh
obliques - in front of rib cage
hamstrings - back of thigh

**Colossians 2:18-19** NKJV "Let no one cheat you of your reward, taking delight in false humility and worship of angels, intruding into those things which he has not seen, vainly puffed up by his fleshly mind, and not holding fast to the Head, from whom all the body, nourished and knit together by joints and ligaments, grows with the increase that is from God."

**Tendons** are connectors. They are made of strong tissue and connect the muscles to the bones. There are thousands of tendons in the human body, and they are made of strong material called collagen, which is a type of protein. They can also weaken as you get older, so eating healthy will keep them strong.

**Joints** are the places where 2 or more bones meet together. Some examples are elbows, wrists, ankles, and shoulders. The biggest joint is in the knee. It connects the kneecap bone, shin bone, and thigh bone. Joints are made of cartilage, and they protect the bones from rubbing together and causing damage. It would be very painful for any two bones to be attached without a joint of cartilage in between them. Cartilage wears down over time, but you can slow this breakdown by eating healthy and getting enough vitamins and minerals.

**Ligaments** are connectors that connect bones to bones at a joint. They look like string or thick rubber bands and are made of collagen. When a ligament is sprained or broken, it can be very painful. The joint will not be able to work until the ligament regrows or is repaired with surgery which can take months of recovery time.

We have two projects for your child to choose from. Pick one to complete for the final presentation in this unit, or do both according to your time and resources.

Project 1: Bones in the Skeletal System

Project 2: Spinal Cord Model and Testing Bone Strength

# Bones in the Skeletal System

**Ephesians 5:30** NKJV "For we are members of His body, of His flesh and of His bones."

God's creation of man is a total miracle. Every bone, joint, muscle, and tendon is fit together to hold all of the organs in place. We can move easily and bend at all of our joints because of the protective cartilage located in them.

When a baby is born, they have 300 bones which are much softer than adult bones. They are flexible and allow the baby to learn how to crawl and walk more easily. By the time a baby is a grown adult, many of the bones have fused together and become stronger. There are 206 bones in every adult. Some bones are stronger than others and can hold up to 3 times the total body weight of a person. Calcium, lifting weights, and eating healthy are the best way to keep bones strong and avoid **osteoporosis**. This is when a person gets older and their bones become weak and brittle.

Scientists use specific scientific names for each of the 206 bones in the body. This is done to avoid confusion. Today, you will draw a sketch of your body and label some of the most well-known bones using their scientific names.

## Materials Needed:

- Skeletal System page(boy or girl)
- scissors
- construction paper
- glue
- color pencils
- pencil and think marker

# Directions:

**First**, cut out the boy or girl Bones in the Skeletal System and the Names of the Bones page.

**Second**, cut out each label from the Names of the Bones page and glue it in the correct place on the Bones of the Skeletal System page. Use the common names below the box to help you glue them in the right place.

**Third**, glue the Bones of the Skeletal System page on a piece of construction paper. Allow all the parts you glued to adequately dry.

**Now**, use your color pencils to color each Bone part a different color.

Save your Bones of the Skeletal System page for the final presentation at the end of this Human Body Unit.

# Names of the Bones

| Cranium |
|---|
Skull

| Mandible |
|---|
Jaw

| Sternum |
|---|
Chest bone

| Scapula |
|---|
Shoulder

| Ribs |
|---|
Ribs

| Vertebrae |
|---|
Backbone

| Ilium |
|---|
Hip

| Humerus |
|---|
Upper Arm

| Radius |
|---|
Lower Arm
thumb side

| Ulna |
|---|
Lower Arm
litter finger side

| Carpals |
|---|
Wrist

| Metacarpal |
|---|
Hand

| Phalanges |
|---|
Fingers

| Femur |
|---|
Thigh

| Patella |
|---|
kneecap

| Tibia |
|---|
Shin

| Fibula |
|---|
Calf

| Tarsal |
|---|
Ankle

| Metatarsal |
|---|
Foot

| Phalanges |
|---|
Toe

# Bones in the Skeletal System

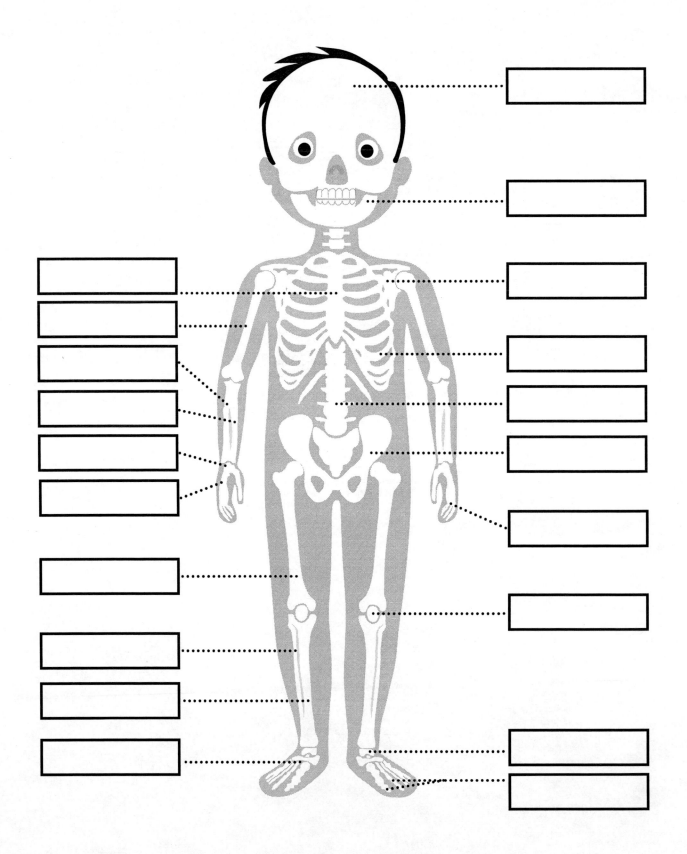

# Bones in the Skeletal System

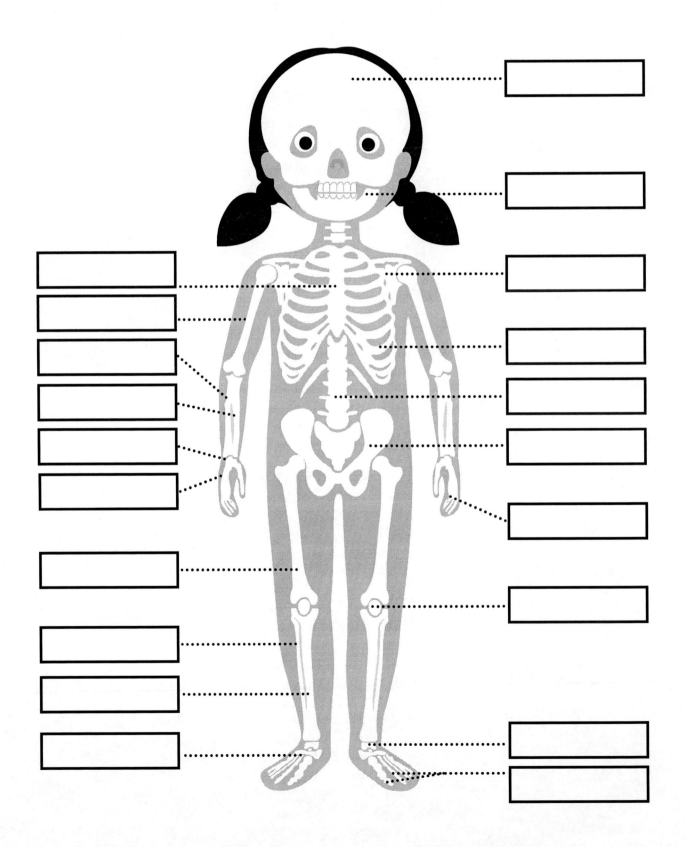

# Spinal Cord Model and Testing Bone Strength

**Proverbs 17:22** NKJV "A merry heart does good, like medicine, but a broken spirit dries the bones."

The bones of the human body contain calcium and are very strong. If 2 bones rubbed together, it would be painful and they could even chip. God put cartilage around every bone to keep them moving easily and free from pain. Cartilage is a smooth substance that helps bones to glide against each other smoothly.

One set of bones which shows this special design very clearly is the vertebrate in the backbone. They are 33 cylinder shaped bones of different lengths and they are all connected by flat disks of cartilage. They are hollow and surround the delicate spinal cord. This cord connects the brain with the rest of the body and helps control all movement of muscles.

Today, you will create a model of the vertebrae that shows the cord, bones, and cartilage disks. Then you will do an activity that shows what happens when calcium is removed from strong bones.

## Spinal Cord Model

## Materials Needed:

- Rigatoni or ziti pasta
- Pipe cleaners
- Gummy life savers

## Directions:

**First**, layout end to end, 33 pieces of rigatoni or ziti pasta cylinders. They can be the same or different lengths. These are your vertebrae bones.

**Second**, attach pipe cleaners to each other until you have a length that is just an inch longer than the pasta chain. This is your spinal cord.

**Third**, string the pasta onto the spinal cord with a gummy ring in between each one. If you have pasta of different lengths, put the shortest on the top and the longest on the bottom. The gummy rings are the cartilage disks. Tie a knot into each end so the pasta doesn't slip off.

Now, hold your model up with the shortest pieces on top. This is a replica of your backbone.

Answer the questions on the Spinal Cord Model page.

# Testing Bone Strength

## Materials Needed:

- Leftover cooked chicken bones
- 2 Cups
- White vinegar
- Water
- Spinal Cord Model and Testing Bone Strength page
- Masking tape
- Marker

## Directions:

**First**, clean off the cooked chicken bones so there is no meat on them. Put a bone or group of bones into 2 different cups.

**Second**, add water to one cup and add vinegar to the other cup, making sure the bones are completely covered.

**Third**, label the cups with masking tape and a marker so you know which is which.

Now, wait 48 hours and then take out the bones and rinse them off in the sink.

Vinegar removes calcium from bones, so you should see a difference between the bones.

Answer the questions on the Testing Bone Strength page.

# Spinal Cord Model

Hold your backbone from the top. Pretending it is your back, try to move it forward and backward like you are bending over to pick something off the floor. What happened?

_____

As you hold the backbone from the top, can you see the spinal cord in between the pasta pieces? Is the cord protected?

_____

Take 2 extra pieces of the pasta and rub and scrape them together strongly. What happened?

_____

## Testing Bone Strength

After washing off the bones, try bending them back and forth.

What happened to the bone in water?

_____

What happens to the bone in vinegar?

_____

Is this what you expected? _____

What does this show you about calcium and bone strength?

_____

## Week 3: The Teeth

God created the human body and all of its parts to work together. Your heart, lungs, brain, stomach, skin, and many other organs are perfectly designed by the Lord. These body parts are made of living cells and so they can **regenerate**. For example, if you get a cut on your skin, it will be able to heal itself if you keep it clean. When you get sick, blood vessels bring white blood cells to that part of the body to heal you. A broken bone can sometimes grow back correctly over time when you keep it completely still and protected in a cast.

There is one part of your body that is not made of living cells and cannot grow back - your teeth. A baby is born without teeth, and then a set of 20 baby teeth grows in around the age of 1-2. These baby teeth fall out and are replaced with 32 adult teeth around 7-8 years old. Once a person's adult teeth grow in, that is their only set. If any of these teeth are lost or damaged, it will take a dentist to fix or replace them. Teeth do not regenerate unless the Lord does a supernatural miracle.

There are several layers under the part of the tooth that we can see. The top, white layer is called the **enamel**. It is the hardest material in the human body. The next layer is **dentin**. It is made of a hard material like a bone and it supports the shape of the tooth. Under the dentin is a soft material called **pulp**. In the pulp are very sensitive nerve endings. If anything ever gets through the enamel and the dentin into the center pulp area of the tooth, it would touch the nerves there and send an immediate signal of pain to the brain.

Our teeth are attached to **gums** which are a pink color and grow around the teeth. They are just as important to keep clean as the teeth. Under the gums and teeth is a very strong material called **cementum** which keeps the teeth attached to the jaw bone.

## Why do I need to brush my teeth and floss?

God created us perfectly and gave us saliva in our mouths to keep our teeth and gums healthy. Each day, any bacteria that gathers on our teeth is washed away by our saliva. When we eat something with sugar in it, the bacteria eats the sugar and it grows faster and stronger. Now it is too hard and sticky for our saliva to wash away. This sticky bacteria on our teeth is called **plaque**. When this plaque stays on our teeth for a long period of time, it can wear away the enamel, and even the dentin eventually. This part of the tooth that is worn away becomes a hole which is called a **cavity**. It is very important to scrub away plaque before it makes a hole and we can do this with regularly brushing teeth. A string of **floss** should be used at least once every day to clean the bacteria and plaque in between the teeth. Cavities can even grow in between teeth. Once a tooth has a cavity, only a dentist can fill in the hole. If this isn't done, it will continue to grow and reach the root. This can be extremely painful and can also lead to the entire tooth falling out.

The easiest way to keep our mouths, teeth, and gums healthy is by brushing with toothpaste every morning and evening and not allowing bacteria to grow and turn into plaque. Even the tongue can grow harmful bacteria so it is recommended to brush that too. We can also limit the amount of sugar we eat and drink. It is a good idea to rinse the mouth out with water after eating a sugary snack, dessert, or drink to wash out any extra sugar particles.

We can also eat foods with vitamin A, vitamin C, and calcium in them which strengthens tooth enamel.

Humans have 4 different types of 32 permanent teeth.

**Incisors** are sharp teeth designed for cutting foods into small pieces. They are located at the front of the mouth, 4 on the top and 4 on the bottom.

**Canines** are sharp teeth that are pointy. They are used to cut the hardest foods like meat. There are 2 on the top and 2 on the bottom.

**Bicuspids** are located next to the canine teeth. They are flat and have ridges in them. They are used for crushing and mashing food. There are 4 on the top and 4 on the bottom.

**Molars** are the largest teeth and they are flat. They can grind food to the smallest particles so it can be digested. There are 6 on the top and 6 on the bottom.

We have two projects for your child to choose from. Pick one to complete for the final presentation in this unit, or do both according to your time and resources.

## Project 1: Egg Brushing Experiment

## Project 2: Anatomy of a Tooth

# Egg Brushing Experiment

**Genesis 49:12** NKJV "His eyes are darker than wine, and his teeth whiter than milk."

The outside white layer of a tooth is made of enamel. This is the hardest material in the human body, but it can wear down over time. If it wears down too much, a cavity can form which is like a hole in the outer layer of the tooth.

The enamel on a tooth is much like the shell on an egg. They have their differences, but they both have a form of calcium in them. Acid and sugar in our foods and drinks break down the calcium in our enamel and wear this coating down. The destruction of enamel is proportional to the level of acid and sugar in the food or drink.

Today, you will simulate what happens when certain ingredients in drinks sit on the enamel of your teeth for a long time.

## Materials Needed:

- 3 Cups
- 3 White hard boiled eggs
- 1 Cup lemonade
- 1 Cup soda (brown in color like cola or root beer)
- Toothbrush
- Toothpaste
- Egg Brushing Experiment page

## Directions:

**First**, fill 1 cup with the water, 1 cup with the lemonade, and 1 cup with the soda.

**Second**, add a hard boiled egg to each cup and wait 24 hours.

**Third**, one at a time brush each egg with the toothbrush and water. Write down your observations on the Egg Brushing Experiment page.

**Fourth**, one at a time brush each egg with the toothbrush and toothpaste. Write down your observations on the Egg Brushing Experiment page.

Keep your finished Egg Brushing Experiment page for your final presentation at the end of this Human Body Unit.

# Egg Brushing Experiment

Name: _____ Date: _____

What I think will happen during my experiment:

_____

What did the egg look like? Did the stain come off?

Egg in water:

_____

Egg in lemonade:

_____

Egg in soda:

_____

Which liquid did the most damage to the eggshell?
Was it easy to fix? What did I learn?

_____

# Anatomy of a Tooth

**Psalm 139:14** NKJV "I will praise You, for I am fearfully and wonderfully made; marvelous are Your works, and that my soul knows very well."

The crown of a tooth is the very top part you can see. It contains enamel and the layer of dentin underneath. The dentin layer absorbs heat and cold so any extreme temperatures don't reach the nerve endings.

The next layer is the neck of a tooth. It starts where the tooth and the gums meet and is the middle layer. It contains some dentin, pulp, and nerve endings.

The bottom layer of a tooth is the root. This is actually almost 70% of the tooth and it is the part that is never seen and attached to the jawbone. It contains the roots and cementum which is very strong and keeps our teeth from moving around.

Today, you will cut out and glue the different parts of a tooth to a poster. Then you will label each part.

## Materials Needed:

- Construction paper (pink, blue, white and yellow)
- Anatomy of a Tooth template pages
- Pencil
- Scissors
- Glue
- String/yarn
- Crayons

# Directions:

**First**, cut out the templates from the Anatomy of a Tooth pages and the oval labels. Keep the oval labels with the descriptions of each part and the title for later.

**Second**, trace the outline of the larger tooth shape onto white construction paper. Trace the medium shape onto yellow paper. Trace the smallest shape onto white construction paper. Cut out all three shapes.

**Third**, cut a piece of pink construction paper in half across its width. Glue this down onto the blue construction paper so you have a paper that is blue on top and pink on the bottom. The pink part of the construction paper is the gums.

**Fourth**, glue the large white tooth onto the construction paper, so the markings on the sides are at the gum line. About half of the tooth should be in the gums, and half will be above the gums. Make sure the bottom slit of the white tooth is all pink.

**Fifth**, glue the yellow dentin onto the tooth so it is centered. Glue the smallest white piece on top of the yellow dentin shape.

**Next**, use your crayons to draw in little roots that look like tree branches on the smallest white shape that is showing in the middle of the dentin. These are your nerve endings in the pulp.

**Now**, cut 2 pieces of string about 6 inches long each and glue on each side of the pulp so it goes straight down. The top of the root should start where the gray ovals are on the template. The string roots will hang below the bottom of the tooth because they are connected deep into the gums.

**Finally**, glue the oval labels around the large white tooth. Make a line or glue a piece of string or yarn pointing to the part described.

Save your Anatomy of a Tooth to share in your final presentation at the end of this Human Body unit.

Example:

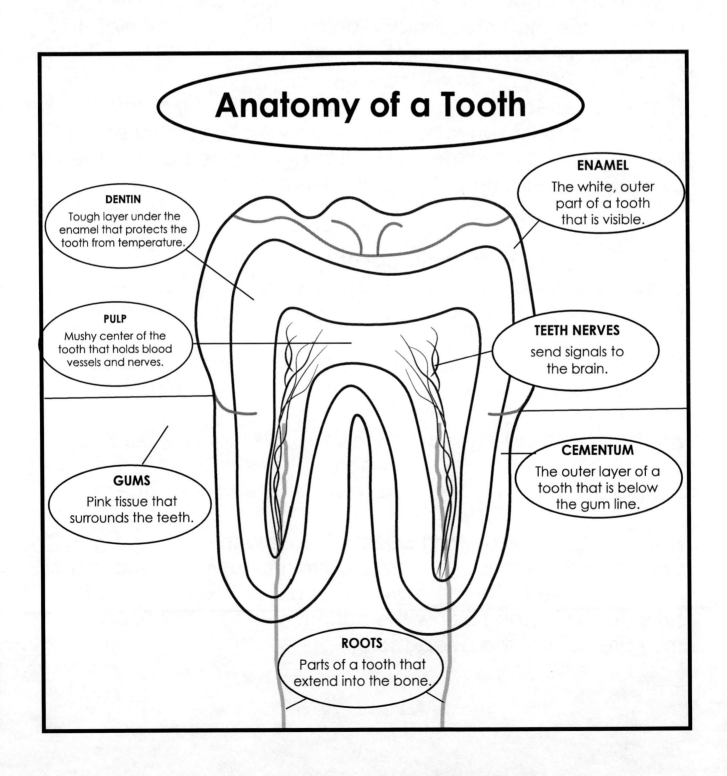

Title:

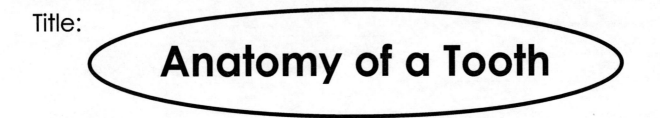

Anatomy of a Tooth

Large tooth template:

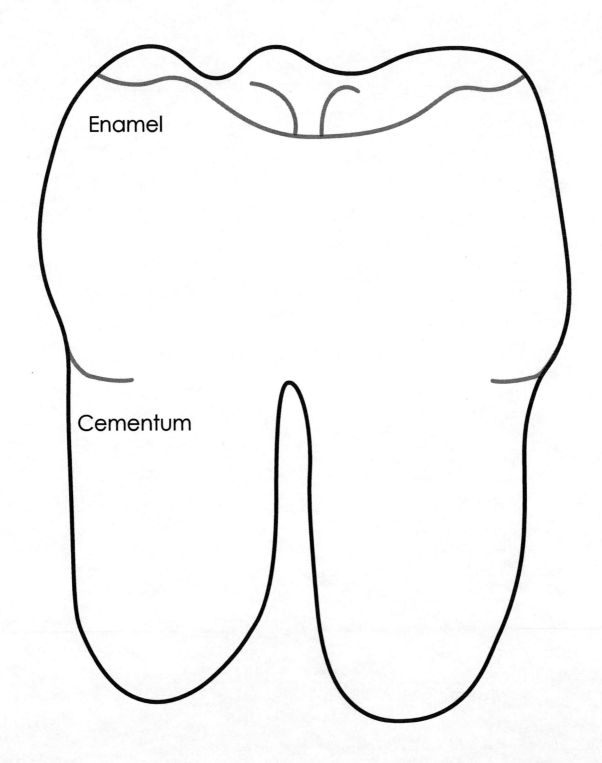

# Anatomy of a Tooth

Medium shape template:

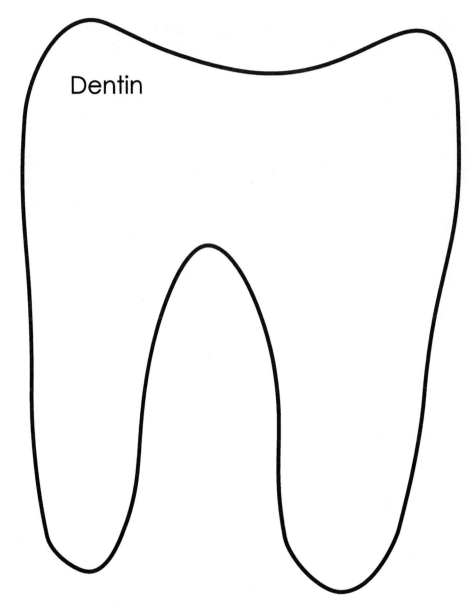

Dentin

Labels:

**DENTIN**

Tough layer under the enamel that protects the tooth from temperature.

**GUMS**

Pink tissue that surrounds the teeth.

# Anatomy of a Tooth

Smallest shape template:

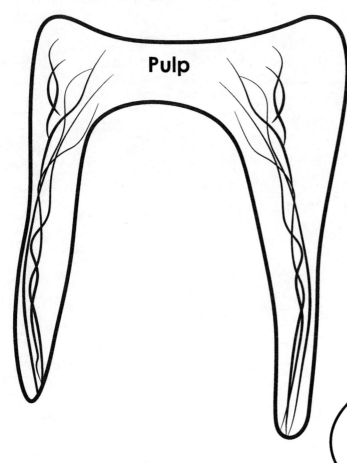

Labels:

**PULP**

Mushy center of the tooth that holds blood vessels and nerves.

**ENAMEL**

The white, outer part of a tooth that is visible.

**CEMENTUM**

The outer layer of a tooth that is below the gum line.

**TEETH NERVES**

send signals to the brain.

**ROOTS**

Parts of a tooth that extend into the bone.

# Week 4: The Human Body Presentation

**Psalm 139:14** NKJV "I will praise You, for I am fearfully and wonderfully made; marvelous are Your works, and that my soul knows very well."

The Lord intricately designed the human body to work with many different parts all connected together. You learned about some of these specific parts in this unit. This is called the study of anatomy.

Humans have 5 senses, and 1 of them is hearing. The ears pick up signals and send them to the brain to be translated. There are many minuscule parts to the ear, but they each have a crucial part in making sure we can hear and understand things and they also help us with balance. Because God wants to protect us, He created an outer ear with sticky wax to trap any dirt or bacteria from getting into the delicate vibrating bones of the inner ear.

The sounds we hear and make are all based on sound waves. These are vibrations that our brains can read and determine what we are hearing. Our brains are also a crucial part of speaking. We use them to know how much air to breath in and out and how to shape our mouths to make different sounds when we want to talk. God also created the epiglottis at the back of the throat to protect our lungs from food or drink.

You learned about the skeleton and all the many parts of the bones, muscles, joints, tendons, and ligaments. Also, in this body system, every part works together to keep the body moving smoothly. A baby would not be able to be born if they had the strong bones of an adult. So, God gave babies very flexible bones that can move during childbirth. He then fuses some of the bones together to make them strong as the child grows to be an adult.

A human body has very important parts that need protection like the heart and the brain. God built the skeleton around the more delicate parts to keep us safe. Bones are extremely strong and when they are healthy, they keep all of the organs and the spinal cord safe.

You learned about all the parts of a tooth and how we can do our part to keep our teeth healthy and strong. When sugar and acid come in to cause damage, we have saliva and a built in protective layer of enamel to keep the nerve endings of the inner tooth safe.

When you study and learn about the human body, you can see how much God loves you and wants to protect you. He made you in His image and you are His prized creation.

This unit's presentation will give you a chance to show your audience all about the wisdom and love of God when He created man. He is our ultimate protection and safety, and He gave us a body with parts that all work together. We can rest and enjoy His presence, instead of worrying how to eat or breathe or sleep. He has great and mighty things that you can do for Him in this world.

# Preparing Your Presentation

## Materials Needed:

- Trifold or poster board
- Scissors
- Tape/glue
- Pen/pencils
- Crayons/markers
- Pictures and projects from the previous weeks
- Construction paper

## Directions:

Make a trifold or poster board of all your observations about the Human Body from the three previous weeks. Include pictures you took of your projects and the projects you made. You can use the trifold diagram below as an example, but your board is yours to make your own; be creative and have fun. Make sure to include the unit title and the driving question. Then invite a relative or family friend over to present what you found out about the Human Body. Use the checklists on the following pages as a guide to prepare for your presentation.

**Psalm 139:14** NKJV "I will praise You, for I am fearfully and wonderfully made; marvelous are Your works, and that my soul knows very well."

# Unit 4
# Trifold/Board Checklist

I have the UNIT TITLE on my trifold/board.

☐

> ## The Human Body

I have the driving question on my trifold/board.

☐

> ## How does the human body work?

I use pictures, drawings, and props on my trifold/board.

☐

I practice how I am going to use my trifold/board.

☐

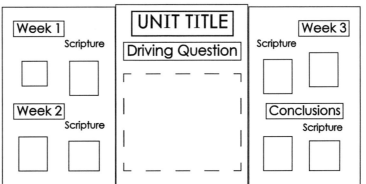

I did my best job on my trifold/board.

☐

# Unit 4
# Presentation Checklist

 I plan what I am going to say for my presentation.

 I practice speaking loud and clear for my presentation.

  I look at my audience during my presentation.

 I answer questions from the audience after my presentation.

 I will do my best on the presentation.

# Unit 5: Health and Manners

| Unit 5: | Driving Question: |
| Health and | How can I take |
| Manners | care of my body? |

# Week 1: Nutrition and Habits

**1 Corinthians 6:19-20** NLT "Don't you realize that your body is the temple of the Holy Spirit, who lives in you and was given to you by God? You do not belong to yourself, for God bought you with a high price. So you must honor God with your body."

Good nutrition and exercise is how you take care of the body that God made for you. When you take care of yourself, you are honoring God.

## What is nutrition?

To explain nutrition, think for a moment about a brand new car. How does the car move? What makes it go? Of course you know that fuel or gasoline is needed for a car to actually work. If you were to put milk or water into the gas tank, it wouldn't move. Even if it was a really nice new car with all perfect parts, it would never work with water in the gas tank; it needs gasoline. Your body is made the same way. God created all the parts of your body and they are made to work together perfectly. But they need fuel in order to keep working. Food is fuel for the human body. Everything we eat and drink to keep the body working well is called nutrition. Good nutrition is eating foods that keep the body healthy, and bad nutrition is eating foods that do not keep the body healthy. Good nutrition fights against sickness, gives you energy, and even helps you learn better.

**Psalm 139:13-14** NLT "You made all the delicate, inner parts of my body and knit me together in my mother's womb. Thank you for making me so wonderfully complex! Your workmanship is marvelous - how well I know it."

## What things should we eat to have good nutrition?

Doctors have studied the human body and nutrition. They have figured out the best combination of foods to eat. For children around 6-10 years old, here is the recommended amount of each food group for each day. These are all estimates and can vary greatly depending on the amount of exercise you have daily. A serving equals about 1/2 cup.

4-5 servings per day of **vegetables** like broccoli and carrots
2-3 servings per day of **fruits** like apples and bananas
3-4 servings per day of **dairy** like cheese and milk
4-5 servings per day of **protein** like chicken, eggs, and nuts
4-5 servings per day of **grains** like pasta, bread, and rice

## Why do we have to eat servings from all these different groups?

Each group above has a different **nutrient** that the body needs. Vegetables have a lot of different **vitamins** and **minerals** in them, depending on what vegetable you are eating. They help blood move easily through your body, and help your brain to send and receive signals. They also strengthen your immune system to fight off germs. They help your organs like the liver and stomach work better.

Fruits have natural sugars which give you energy, and **fiber** which helps your body digest food.

Dairy gives you **vitamin D** and **calcium** which are necessary for strong bones. Dairy can also help fight against high blood pressure and diabetes.

Protein is needed to keep your bones strong and it also gives you energy.

Grains have **carbohydrates** which give you energy to move, play, run, and think.

## Is there anything else we can do to be healthy?

Good nutrition is the first step to a healthy life. Another thing that is just as important is exercise. Anytime you are moving your body, it is exercise. There are so many benefits from exercise:

It keeps your heart strong.
It keeps you at a healthy weight.
It gives you a balanced mood and good attitude.
It helps you sleep soundly at night.
It helps your brain work well.
It helps your food digest.

## What are some things I can do to get exercise?

You can ride your bike, climb a tree, play tag outside, clean your room, go roller skating, play on the playground, walk up and down the stairs, or go for a walk with your family. You should aim to get at least 1 hour of exercise every day, and this can be split up into different pieces throughout your day.

## What is a habit?

A habit is something that you do every day without even having to think about it. It is part of your daily routine. For example, you eat breakfast every morning. This is something that you've always done so it is now just part of your daily routine. You don't have to make a list and remind yourself to eat breakfast. The good news is that you can always make a new habit. Maybe you haven't been eating healthy or getting exercise or reading your Bible every day. If you start today and keep  doing it every day, pretty soon it will become a habit and part of your everyday life. This new habit will come naturally to you and you won't forget to do it.

We have two projects for your child to choose from. Pick one to complete for the final presentation in this unit, or do both according to your time and resources.

Project 1: Food Groups Plate

Project 2: Nutrients for the Body

# Food Groups Plate

**Genesis 9:3** NLT "I have given them to you for food, just as I have given you grain and vegetables."

Calories are units of measurement. They measure the amount of energy coming into the body and going out. Calories enter into the body through food. Every food has a different number of calories in it. Foods like doughnuts and cake have more calories than fruit or vegetables. Calories go out of a body by moving and by activity. Even sleeping and breathing are activities that burns calories. The more strenuous the exercise, the more calories that are burned.

Every day, the amount of calories going in and going out should be near the same number, unless someone is trying to gain or lose weight. For a child around 6-10 years old, the average calories going in and out is between 1200-1800 each day. The number of calories can be found on packaged food labels and on many websites and apps. Scientists and doctors have also made suggested amounts of foods children should be eating each day from each of the 5 food groups.

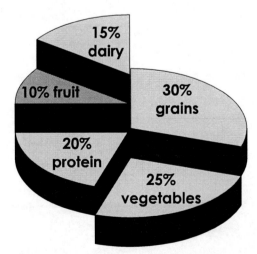

These amounts are all approximate and based on the average activity level of children today.

Today, you will make a helpful Food Groups Plate to show how much of each food you should be eating every day. It will look like a pie chart which divides up the total food you eat in one whole day.

## Materials Needed:

- Pie Food Group page
- Paper plate
- Construction paper
- Scissors
- Pencil
- Color pencils and markers
- Glue
- Magazines and catalogs

## Directions:

**First**, cut out the pie shape for the Pie Food Group page and cut apart each piece. Cut out the labels for each piece too.

**Second**, trace each pie piece onto colored construction paper. Make sure each piece is a different color. Cut the traced pieces out.

**Third**, glue each pie piece onto the paper plate. The pie should fit together on the paper plate. Glue the labels on each piece.

**Fourth**, cut out and glue pictures of different foods from recipe magazines or catalogs. Make sure you have at least one for each food group. You can also draw the food in each pie piece.

Save your Food Groups Plate for your final presentation at the end of this Health and Manners Unit.

# Pie Food Group

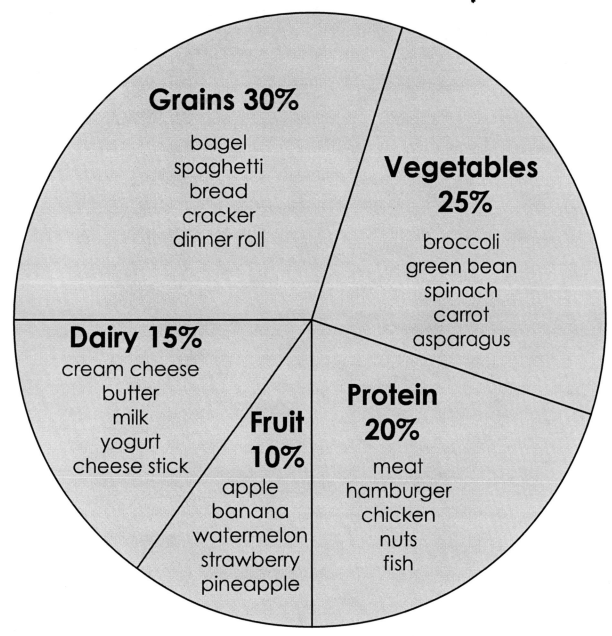

**Grains 30%**

bagel
spaghetti
bread
cracker
dinner roll

**Vegetables 25%**

broccoli
green bean
spinach
carrot
asparagus

**Dairy 15%**

cream cheese
butter
milk
yogurt
cheese stick

**Fruit 10%**

apple
banana
watermelon
strawberry
pineapple

**Protein 20%**

meat
hamburger
chicken
nuts
fish

Labels:

**Protein 20%**
4 - 5 Servings a day

**Fruit 10%**
2 - 3 Servings a day

**Grains 30%**
4 - 5 Servings a day

**Dairy 15%**
3 - 4 Servings a day

**Vegetables 25%**
4 - 5 Servings a day

# Nutrients for the Body

**Genesis 1:29** NLT "Then God said, "Look! I have given you every seed-bearing plant throughout the earth and all the fruit trees for your food.""

Whenever you eat something healthy, you are putting vitamins and minerals into your body. Some of the foods we eat don't have any vitamins or minerals in them. An example of this is cookies and candy. But the 5 main food groups you learned about in this lesson each have different vitamins and minerals in them. Your body needs a lot of different foods to get all the vitamins you need. Your mom or dad might also give you extra vitamins to help you get everything your body needs to be healthy.

Today, you will read about which vitamins and minerals help all of your different body parts. You will also research and write what foods are a good source of each vitamin and mineral you need.

There is a lot of overlap with vitamins and foods. For example, Vitamin A helps the eyes to see better, and it also makes our bones stronger. For this project, we will research on the Internet or from books at your local library about food sources for specific vitamins.

## Materials Needed:

- Nutrients for the Body pages
- Pencil and glue
- Books about vitamins and minerals or Internet
- Scissors
- Construction paper

## Directions:

**First**, cut out the Nutrient for the Body pages. Read how each vitamin and mineral helps different parts of your body. Which foods contain these vitamins and minerals?

**Second**, use books or the Internet to find which foods contain each vitamin and mineral.

**Third**, choose three that you like to eat for each vitamin and mineral and write them on the lines provided.

**Now**, glue this onto a piece of construction paper. Hang this on your refrigerator or in the kitchen to help you remember what foods to eat.

Save your Nutrients for the Body project for your final presentation at the end of this Health and Manners Unit.

# Nutrients for the Body

## Vitamin A

is good for the eyes, tissue, skin, immune system, and bones.

_____

_____

_____

## Vitamin B

is good for the energy, brain, blood, and hair.

_____

_____

_____

## Vitamin C

is good for the immune system and blood vessels.

_____

_____

_____

## Vitamin D

is good for the bones and teeth.

_____

_____

_____

## Vitamin E

is good for the brain and muscles.

_____

_____

_____

## Vitamin K

is good for blood clotting.

_____

_____

_____

# Nutrients for the Body

## Calcium

is good for the
bones, teeth, muscles, and
blood pressure.

_____

_____

_____

## Iron

is good for the
lungs, hormones, and
red blood cells.

_____

_____

_____

## Magnesium

is good for the
heart, blood, and bones.

_____

_____

_____

## Potassium

is good for the
heart, muscles, and bones.

_____

_____

_____

## Zinc

is good for the
liver, immune system, and
healing wounds.

_____

_____

_____

## Fiber

is a carbohydrate that
helps us digest food.

_____

_____

_____

# Week 2: Cleanliness and Hygiene

**Psalm 51:10** NLT "Create in me a clean heart, O God. Renew a loyal spirit within me."

Another way to stay healthy and take care of the body is by staying clean. Cleanliness is keeping the body clean by practicing good **hygiene**. Hygiene makes you look nice, but more importantly, it keeps germs away.

## What are germs?

**Germs** are living organisms. They are so small that they can only be seen under a microscope. Thousands of germs could all fit together on a pencil eraser. A germ is either a **virus** or **bacteria**.

## What is a virus?

A virus is a tiny particle that has no life until it has entered a living cell in a plant or animal or human. They are all around us. A virus can enter a body when someone breathes it in or touches a surface that has a virus on it. Once inside the body, it comes alive and starts to split and multiply very quickly. Some examples of viruses are colds, flu, measles, and chicken pox. A human has a great defense system against viruses, it is the **immune system**. It sends **white blood cells** to the site of the virus to kill it. The stronger the immune system, the quicker the virus can be beaten. Once the white blood cells fight off a virus, they remember it well. They have an incredible memory. If that same virus tries to come back, it will be removed even faster. Vaccines are weak pieces of viruses that are put into the body to train the immune system to fight against them.

Then if the virus does come, the white blood cells already know it and can fight it off more quickly and easily.

## What is bacteria?

Bacteria are microscopic, living organisms that are found in the body, ground, food, air, and all around us. Most bacteria are actually healthy, and a small amount are harmful. Harmful bacteria are called **pathogens**. Some examples of pathogens are typhoid fever, leprosy, food poisoning, and pneumonia. Bad bacteria in the body can cause stomach aches, headaches, tiredness, nausea, constipation, rashes, and chest pain.
Good bacteria in the body helps break down food and helps with the entire digestion process. Good bacteria in the earth helps break down dead plants and animals and uses these materials in our soil.

## How can we get rid of pathogens in the body?

There are 3 ways to fight off pathogens. Some people take antibiotics which is medicine that a doctor will prescribe. Another way to remove pathogens is by increasing the amount of good bacteria in the body. This can happen by eating a wide variety of healthy foods and vegetables. Good bacteria can kill bad bacteria. Another way is by practicing good hygiene.

## What is good hygiene?

Good hygiene is keeping the body clean and healthy. Doing this every day will fight off many viruses and bacteria, and it is so important. Washing your body and hands keeps bacteria and viruses off of you and the food you will eat. It keeps you from spreading a virus to someone else too when you touch them or their things. Sneezing or coughing into the air can spread any germs you have onto other people.

## Some examples of good hygiene are:

Washing hands before eating or cooking or touching food
Washing hands after using the bathroom
Wearing clean clothes
Washing hair
Washing the body
Brushing and flossing teeth 2 times per day
Getting enough sleep
Not sharing cups, utensils, or hats with others
Coughing and sneezing into the elbow and not into the air

When you do all of these things, you will protect yourself from many viruses and bacteria that are trying to infect you. Eating healthy will help your immune system to be strong and fight off any germs that do get into your body.

## Did You Know?

There was a time in Europe in the 1300s when people did not practice good hygiene. They didn't know that it was important and so they didn't bathe or wash their hands before cooking and eating. Scientists hadn't learned about germs yet. Because of the bad hygiene, there was a huge plague called the Bubonic Plague that killed almost 200 million people. This will not happen today because now people know how important it is to have good hygiene.

# Is there anything else we need to keep clean?

Even more important than the body, we need to keep our hearts clean. This means that we fight off any sin germs that try to come in. The Bible tells us that sin starts in our thoughts. For example, we might feel a thought of anger about someone. This can turn into sin if we let it stay in our mind. We might end up yelling at them or hitting them. To keep the heart clean and pure, we can take that thought and submit it to the Lord. We can confess that we have anger and ask Him to remove it. We can rebuke that angry thought and tell it to leave in the name of Jesus. No evil thought or spirit can stay near Jesus' name.

**2 Corinthians 10:4-5** NKJV "For the weapons of our warfare are not carnal but mighty in God for pulling down strongholds, casting down arguments and every high thing that exalts itself against the knowledge of God, bringing every thought into captivity to the obedience of Christ."

A clean and pure heart is when we submit to God throughout the day and confess any thoughts or sins to Him.

**Matthew 5:8** NLT "God blesses those whose hearts are pure, for they will see God."

We have two projects for your child to choose from. Pick one to complete for the final presentation in this unit, or do both according to your time and resources.

Project 1: Personal Hygiene Chart

Project 2: Spreading Germs Experiments

# Personal Hygiene Chart

**Ephesians 5:29** NKJV "For no one ever hated his own flesh, but nourishes and cherishes it, just as the Lord does the church."

When you take care of your body and keep it clean, you are honoring the Lord. He created you and loves you so much. He doesn't want to see you get sick from the germs all around you. He made your body and wants you to take care of His creation. So when you keep yourself clean, eat healthy, and exercise, you are being a good steward of the one body God gave you to take care of. When you feel healthy and strong, you can do great things for God and serve Him mightily. You will not be losing time with sickness and disease. You can pray for others and His kingdom more when you're not praying for healing for yourself. Now, you will get sick sometimes, that is part of living on this Earth. But we can all do our part to keep ourselves as healthy as possible and make times of sickness a rare thing. God wants you to live a healthy life, free from sickness.

**John 10:10** NKJV "The thief does not come except to steal, and to kill, and to destroy. I have come that they may have life, and that they may have it more abundantly."

Today, you will create a Personal Hygiene Chart to track your daily activities. Once you do this for several weeks, these activities will become habits. You will be able to do all of them without thinking about it. They will be automatic.

## Materials Needed:

- Personal Hygiene Chart
- Personal Hygiene Activities page
- Tape

- Scissors
- Color pencils
- Page protector
- Dry erase marker
- Glue

## Directions:

**First**, cut out the Personal Hygiene Chart and write your name at the top.

**Second**, cut out the Personal Hygiene Activities page. Pick out 5 of the activities you want to focus on this week. Then color and cut out each box.

**Third**, glue the activity boxes to the left side of the Personal Hygiene Chart.

**Now**, put the chart into a page protector. Tape this on the wall in your room or bathroom. Make sure to put it somewhere you will see it every day.

**Next**, use a dry erase marker to put a check mark or smiley face into each box to check off when you have completed that activity each day. At the end of the week, look at your chart. How did you do? Now you can erase all the check marks and start over with your chart for the next week.

Save your Personal Hygiene Chart for your final presentation at the end of this Health and Manners Unit.

# Personal Hygiene Chart for _____

| Activity | SUN | MON | TUE | WED | THUR | FRI | SAT |
|---|---|---|---|---|---|---|---|
|  |  |  |  |  |  |  |  |
|  |  |  |  |  |  |  |  |
|  |  |  |  |  |  |  |  |
|  |  |  |  |  |  |  |  |
|  |  |  |  |  |  |  |  |

# Personal Hygiene Activities

**Brush My Teeth**

**Brush My Hair**

**Put On Deodorant**

**Take a Bath**

**Read My Bible**

**Wash My Hands**

**Talk to God**

**Put Dirty Clothes in Hamper**

**Wash My Hair**

**Wash My Face**

# Personal Hygiene Chart for _____

| Activity | SUN | MON | TUE | WED | THUR | FRI | SAT |
|---|---|---|---|---|---|---|---|
|  |  |  |  |  |  |  |  |
|  |  |  |  |  |  |  |  |
|  |  |  |  |  |  |  |  |
|  |  |  |  |  |  |  |  |
|  |  |  |  |  |  |  |  |

# Spreading Germs Experiments

**Hebrews 10:22** NKJV "let us draw near with a true heart in full assurance of faith, having our hearts sprinkled from an evil conscience and our bodies washed with pure water."

Germs are all around us, and they are invisible. They spread very fast, especially when people are not washing their hands with soap. Rinsing hands with just water will not kill the viruses and bacteria on them. If hands are not washed before preparing food, then the viruses and bacteria on our hands will be on all the food that is served. This will affect all the people that eat it. Germs also spread very quickly in the air. Coughing and sneezing into the air around us is very dangerous. Other people will breathe in this contaminated air. Coughing into the elbow will ensure that germs land on our clothing and not in the air so they will not affect others. Today, you will choose **one or more** of the following activities to see how germs spread so quickly and easily.

# Donut Germs

## Materials Needed:

- White powdered donut
- Spreading Germs Experiment page
- Pencil
- Color pencils or crayons

## Directions:

**First**, hold a powdered donut in your hands. Move it from hand to hand. **Second**, gently blow on the donut into the air.

**Third**, take a bite of the donut and wipe your mouth on your sleeve.

**Next**, pick up one of your toys or any other item.

**Now**, hug your mom or sibling.

**Finally**, look around. Do you see white powder on anything? Are there any crumbs on the floor or table?

This is how germs are. They spread to everything we touch. They are not easily removed. Take some time to clean the powder off of everything.

Fill out the Spreading Germs Experiment page. Draw and color a picture of your experiment.

Save your Spreading Germs Experiment page for your final presentation at the end of this Health and Manners Unit.

# Pepper Germs

## Materials Needed:

- 1 Teaspoon black pepper
- Spreading Germs Experiment page
- Pencil
- Color pencils or crayons
- Bowl
- Water
- Dish soap

## Directions:

**First**, fill a bowl with water.

**Second**, sprinkle the pepper over the top of the water. These are germs.

**Third**, spread a lot of dish soap all over your finger and dip it into the water.

The pepper scatters away from your finger. The soap has broken up the water molecules and caused the germs to leave. This shows how soap on your skin can drive germs away.

Wash your hands and clean up any mess.

Fill out the Spreading Germs Experiment page. Draw and color a picture of your experiment.

Save your Spreading Germs Experiment page for your final presentation at the end of this Health and Manners Unit.

# Apple Germs

## Materials Needed:

- One apple cut into three equal pieces
- Spreading Germs Experiment page
- Construction paper
- Glue
- Scissors
- Crayons
- 3 Jars with lids
- Masking tape and marker

## Directions:

**First**, cut the apple into 3 equal pieces. Put one piece immediately into a jar without touching it by sliding it in using a clean utensil. Put the lid on the jar. Label it, No Hands, with masking tape.

After playing outside for awhile and getting dirty, wipe your hands all over the second apple piece, put it into a jar, and cover with the lid. Label it, Dirty Hands, with masking tape.

**Next**, wash your hands very well with soap. Then wipe them all over the last apple piece and put it into the last jar and cover with the lid. Label it, Washed Hands, with masking tape.

Each day, look at the three apple specimens. After about a week, you should see a huge difference in how much bacteria is growing on each apple. Which one is the cleanest? Which one is the dirtiest? What does this tell you about how many germs are on our clean and dirty hands?

Fill out the Spreading Germs Experiment page. Draw and color a picture of your experiment.

# Glitter Germs

## Materials Needed:

- Jar of glitter
- Spreading Germs Experiment page
- Pencil
- Color pencils and crayons
- Hand sanitizer

## Directions:

**First**, spread hand sanitizer all over your hands so they are slightly damp.

**Second**, add a small amount of glitter to your hands. Rub the glitter all over your hands like you are washing them with glitter.

Now is the fun and messy part. Shake hands with a family member, hug them, touch some things around your house, and touch your face (not your eyes).

Now look around. Where do you see glitter? It is probably everywhere! This glitter is just like germs: they spread very easily, and they are very hard to clean up. Now work on cleaning the glitter off of everything. It will take a lot of time and energy to do this. This shows that it is easier to avoid germs in the beginning than it is to clean them up after they have paid a visit.

Fill out the Spreading Germs Experiment page. Draw and color a picture of your experiment.

Save your Spreading Germs Experiment page for your final presentation at the end of this Health and Manners Unit.

# Spreading Germs Experiment

Name: _____ Date: _____

Name of Experiment _____

What I think will happen during my experiment:

Here is a picture of my experiment:

What were the results of my experiment? What did I learn?

# Spreading Germs Experiment

Name: _____     Date: _____

Name of Experiment _____

What I think will happen during my experiment:

What were the results of my experiment? What did I learn?

## Week 3: Respect, Courtesy, Kindness, Thankfulness, Thoughtfulness

**2 Corinthians 4:16** NKJV "Therefore we do not lose heart. Even though our outward man is perishing, yet the inward man is being renewed day by day."

**Galatians 5:22-24** NKJV "But the fruit of the Spirit is love, joy, peace, long-suffering, kindness, goodness, faithfulness, gentleness, self-control. Against such there is no law. And those who are Christ's have crucified the flesh with its passions and desires."

The Bible tells us that when we spend time with the Lord, it changes us. When the Holy Spirit comes into a person, He changes them from the inside out. When we read the Bible and worship God and talk to Him, we are renewed every day into who God wants us to be.

When a farmer plants an apple seed, then an apple tree will grow in that place. In the same way, when we plant seeds of God's word into our hearts, the fruit of those seeds are holy and godly traits as mentioned above in Galatians 5.

**Isaiah 55:11** NKJV "So shall My word be that goes forth from My mouth; it shall not return to Me void, but it shall accomplish what I please, and it shall prosper in the thing for which I sent it."

God's word always bears fruit. The result of time with God will always be godly traits.

# What is a godly trait?

A **trait** is an adjective to describe a person. What are they like? They might have a trait of being tall. Or being happy. Some godly traits are listed in Galatians 5. Some other godly traits are respect, courtesy, kindness, thankfulness, and thoughtfulness. When a person has these godly traits, it is called having good **manners**. They live in a manner that brings glory to God.

## What is respect?

**Respect** is when you honor somebody or something. For example, if you respect the rules of the library, it means that you don't go in the library and start running or yelling. This is not respectful to the rules that are set for that place. Respect means that you understand the rules that are in place and so you follow them. You might really want to run and yell and play, but you understand that it would not be the right thing to do at that time. You **submit** yourself to the **authority** of the rules. If you respect a person, it means you understand that they are somebody that God created and loves with all of His heart. Even if they do something that you don't agree with, you can still honor them by listening to them, especially if they are in authority over you. Some people are very easy to respect, and others are more difficult. But we have to obey God and respect all people because He created them. We submit to God's will and plan for our lives and trust that He put certain people in authority over us.

## What is courtesy?

**Courtesy** is when you are polite to other people. You might hold the door open for someone, or let them go first in line. You use the words "please," "thank you," "yes, ma'am," and "yes, sir." When someone speaks to you, you look them in the eyes and smile, and respond. Having courtesy is having good manners.

## What is kindness?

**Kindness** is when you do an action for somebody that blesses them. Some examples are writing a note to encourage someone or baking them cookies. You could tell a veteran or policeman that you appreciate them. You could help carry someone's groceries or rake leaves for a neighbor. You could see someone who looks sad and tell them that Jesus loves them and pray for them. Kindness happens when we stop thinking about ourselves and start focusing on people around us.

## What is thankfulness?

**Thankfulness** is when you are thankful for what you have. The Bible tells us that we are to thank God all throughout the day for everything. This is His will for us and it will bring us peace and joy. When we are thankful, it brings us into God's presence and brings Him glory. When we are thankful, we are focusing on what we have and realizing that all of it is a gift from God. We do not focus on things we don't have.

## What is thoughtfulness?

**Thoughtfulness** is thinking about other people and their interests. For example, you might have a friend who loves horses. If you see a picture of a horse in a book, you could bring it to show them or lend to them. If you are at the store and see your dad's favorite candy, you could buy it to surprise him later.

## Isn't it hard to have all these godly traits and good manners all of the time?

If you try to live with good manners all the time and decide to live only with godly traits, it's not only hard...it's impossible! We can't do anything on our own without God's help. If you wake up and start every day reading the Bible, listening to worship music, and talking to Jesus, you will probably have most of these traits without even trying. This is true for both children and parents. Any of the traits you don't have, you can practice and learn. The Lord will help you and mold your character into who He created you to be.

## What if I have not been respectful, courteous, kind, thankful, or thoughtful? I forgot to use my manners today.

Nobody is perfect. We have all had times where these godly traits were not in us. Repent and ask God for forgiveness. He will welcome you with open arms. Then ask the Lord to help you. Spend time with Him and Holy Spirit. Godly traits are only hard to have when they are done in your own strength. When you are focused on God and spending time with Him, they will flow more naturally out of you.

**1 John 1:9** NKJV "If we confess our sins, He is faithful and just to forgive us our sins and to cleanse us from all unrighteousness."

We have two projects for your child to choose from. Pick one to complete for the final presentation in this Health and Manners Unit, or do both according to your time and resources.

## Project 1: Help a Neighbor

## Project 2: Thank You Letter

# Help a Neighbor

**Mark 12:30-31** NKJV "'And you shall love the Lord your God with all your heart, with all your soul, with all your mind, and with all your strength.' This is the first commandment. And the second, like it, is this: 'You shall love your neighbor as yourself.' There is no other commandment greater than these."

Jesus taught His followers about the good Samaritan. He used this parable to explain that loving yourself and your neighbor was the most important of all the commandments. When Jesus used the word neighbor, he was talking about anyone that we come into contact with. Today you will make a plan to complete a volunteer kindness for someone and show God's love to them.

## Materials Needed:

- Pen or pencil
- Help a Neighbor  Brainstorming page
- Help a Neighbor Discussion page

## Directions:

**First**, pray and ask God to give you some creative ideas. Now sit down with a parent and the Help a Neighbor Brainstorming page. Read through and answer the questions as best you can.

**Second**, choose one or more of the ideas you come up with and go ask your neighbor if you can help them with one of these ideas or anything else they need. Pray before having this conversation and God will help you have courage. They might come up with an idea that you don't have on your paper.

**Third**, set a time to help them and make sure you have parent approval. Be on time to help and work hard at the task.

**Finally**, fill out the Help a Neighbor Discussion page once you have finished the task.

Keep your finished Help a Neighbor Discussion page to share in your final presentation at the end of this Health and Manners Unit.

# Help a Neighbor Brainstorming

List some of the people in your life or neighborhood who you know and who you think you could help:

_____

_____

_____

With a parent, read through this list and cross out the things that you cannot do (maybe due to weather, time, ability, or money):

| | | |
|---|---|---|
| raking leaves | shoveling snow | pulling weeds |
| walking dog | washing dishes | carrying groceries |
| going to store for a few items | baking cookies | making dinner |
| taking out trash | cleaning/vacuuming | |

Talk to your neighbor and see if they have any ideas for anything they might need help with this week. For example, ask them if you could bring over dinner one night this week or take their dog on a walk for them. You can tell them you are working on a school project about kindness and loving your neighbor.

What will you do for them? _____

_____

When will you do it?_____

_____

# Help a Neighbor Discussion

Name: _____    Date: _____

### Who did you help this week?
### Draw a picture of you and your neighbor.

### What did you do for your neighbor?

_____

_____

### How did you feel after being helpful? How did your neighbor feel? Do you want to do this again?

_____

_____

_____

_____

_____

# Thank You Letter

**Psalm 100:4** NKJV "Enter his gates with thanksgiving, and his courts with praise! Give thanks to him; bless his name!"

The Bible is clear that when we are thankful, a lot of good things happen. We have peace. God is glorified. We are not worried or anxious. We are brought into God's presence. We will feel Him close to us. Thanking God for everything we have brings a feeling of joy to our hearts. You can thank God for your family, your home, your friends, your brain, your health, your church, or anything else you can think of. Everything you have is a gift from God.

**James 1:17** NKJV "Every good gift and every perfect gift is from above, and comes down from the Father of lights, with whom there is no variation or shadow of turning."

It is important to thank people as well as thank God. God put people in your life who have helped you. He never wants us to take them for granted. Today, you will write a thank you letter to someone who has been a blessing in your life.

## Materials Needed:

- Thank You Letter template page
- Thank You Letter Brainstorming page
- Lined paper
- Pen or pencil
- Envelope and stamp

## Directions:

**First**, with a parent, fill out the Thank You Letter Brainstorming page.

**Second**, using the Thank You Letter template page, write your letter on a piece of lined paper. Each part of the template that is underlined should be changed into your own words to fit your own situation.

The underlined words in the Closing Thoughts section should name a godly trait that your person has. Some words you can use are: faithfulness, kindness, generosity, love, patience, joy, thoughtfulness, or gentleness.

Aim for at least 4-5 sentences total for your letter. Sign your name at the bottom and put it into an envelope.

Next, write their name and address on the envelope and mail it or hand it to them in person if you will see them this week.

Take a picture of your thank you letter and keep this picture to share in your final presentation at the end of this Health and Manners Unit.

# Thank You Letter Brainstorming

Who is someone in your life that has helped you or given you something? Some ideas might be your pastor, kids church teacher, friend, relative, neighbor, coach, or church member.

_____

What did they do to help you or what did they give you?
This will be for your first sentence.

_____

_____

List 2 or 3 specific things they did or about the item they gave.
This will be for your 2nd and 3rd sentence.

_____

_____

_____

Write down your favorite part of what they did or part of the gift.
This will be for your last sentence in the main body paragraph.

_____

_____

What godly trait did they have when they helped you?
This will be for your sentence in the closing thoughts paragraph.

_____

_____

(love, faithfulness, kindness, generosity, patience, thoughtfulness)

# Thank You Letter Template

Dear Pastor Pete,
(Greeting)

Thank you so much for <u>teaching me all about God this year.</u> You <u>were very patient with all of us and answered all of our questions.</u> You <u>always brought such fun games and props that made Sunday School so much fun.</u> My favorite part was <u>when you put all the toothpaste on the floor and we had to try and put it back in the tube.</u> That was so much fun!
(Main Body Paragraph)

Thank you again for your <u>faithfulness to serve God at our church.</u> I appreciate you.
(Closing Thoughts)

Sincerely,

<u>Lucy Hunter</u>
(Signature)

| Unit 5: Health and Manners | Driving Question: How can I take care of my body? |

# Week 4: Health and Manners Presentation

**1 Corinthians 6:19-20** NLT "Don't you realize that your body is the temple of the Holy Spirit, who lives in you and was given to you by God? You do not belong to yourself, for God bought you with a high price. So you must honor God with your body."

You have learned so much in this unit about the inside and the outside of your body. You have been given a great gift from the Lord of a spirit, soul, and body. He gave you this one body to take care of and you have learned what it means to be a good steward of it.

Being a good steward means that God created you and God is allowing you to use the body He gave you. It is up to you to do your best to care for your body and spirit. You take care of your body by eating well, exercising, and staying clean. You can take care of your spirit by spending time with the Lord, talking to Him, reading the Bible, and listening to what He is telling you. You can allow God to use you to bless other people. When you live by the power of the Holy Spirit, the fruits of the Spirit will be seen in your life, including respect, courtesy, kindness, thankfulness, and thoughtfulness.

All of this may seem hard to do on your own strength, so we can always ask God to help us be good stewards and honor Him.

You learned about all the different vitamins and minerals that are found in foods. Each vitamin affects a different part of the body, and some vitamins affect many parts. Eating a variety of healthy foods can help you be a good steward of your body. God also created us to move our bodies every day and this keeps us healthy and strong.

You learned about the importance of good hygiene and how to fight off germs of bacteria and germs of viruses. They can spread like wildfire, but we have a great defense against them which is the immune system God gave us. Keeping our hands and bodies clean, especially before we touch food, is so important to our overall health and a very easy way to kill germs before they get in.

This unit's presentation will give you a chance to show your audience all about stewardship of our insides and outsides. We should care for ourselves in body and in spirit. You can explain and show how God gave us ways to steward the bodies He gave us, through eating, exercise, and cleanliness. When we spend time with Him, we see the fruit of that relationship in our manners and our attitudes. Walking with Holy Spirit and in His power always leads to a peaceful life with godly traits.

# Preparing Your Presentation

## Materials Needed:

- Trifold or poster board
- Scissors
- Tape/glue
- Pen/pencils
- Crayons/markers
- Pictures and projects from the previous weeks
- Construction paper

## Directions:

Make a trifold or poster board of all your observations about Health and Manners from the three previous weeks. Include pictures you took of your projects and the projects you made. You can use the trifold diagram below as an example, but your board is yours to make your own; be creative and have fun. Make sure to include the unit title and the driving question. Then invite a relative or family friend over to present what you found out about Health and Manners. Use the checklists on the following pages as a guide to prepare for your presentation.

**1 Corinthians 6:19-20** NLT "Don't you realize that your body is the temple of the Holy Spirit, who lives in you and was given to you by God? You do not belong to yourself, for God bought you with a high price. So you must honor God with your body."

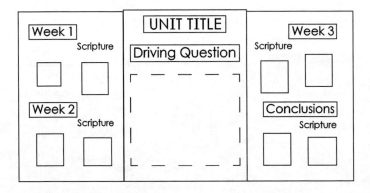

# Unit 5
# Trifold/Board Checklist

I have the UNIT TITLE on my trifold/board.

### Health and Manners

I have the driving question on my trifold/board.

### How can I take care of my body?

I use pictures, drawings, and props on my trifold/board.

I practice how I am going to use my trifold/board.

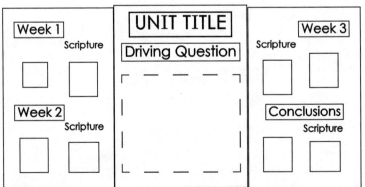

I did my best job on my trifold/board.

# Unit 5
# Presentation Checklist

 I plan what I am going to say for my presentation.

 I practice speaking loud and clear for my presentation.

  I look at my audience during my presentation.

 I answer questions from the audience after my presentation.

 I will do my best on the presentation.

# Unit 6:
# Safety

## Week 1: Safety at Home

Proverbs 18:10 NKJV "The name of the Lord is a strong tower; The righteous run to it and are safe."

Safety is when we are living protected from danger. As believers, God is the ultimate source of safety always. His Word tells us that He will never leave or forsake His children. We are covered by His blood and no weapon formed against us can prosper.

Along with the God-given safety we all have, there is something called wisdom. We can be smart and live in a careful way so we don't take His protection for granted. Here are some ways we can practice safe living at home:

### Safety in the Kitchen

Make sure to never touch the top of the stove. Even if it has been turned off, the burners could still be hot and burn you.

Don't touch knives even if they look safe, because they can cut you. Any chopping with a knife should be done with parental supervision. Always load knives into the dishwasher with the blade pointed down. Scissors are also very sharp. Make sure to walk, and not run with scissors or a knife. When handing them to someone, put the blade in your hand and the handle out.

Wash hands before doing any cooking or touching any food. In general, don't run or play in the kitchen. You also want to watch out for any pot handles on the stove and keep them pointing in toward the wall and not pointing out where they can be bumped and possibly spilled. Use oven mitts to take anything out of the oven, and use 2 hands when carrying serving dishes or baking pans. Never leave anything cooking on the stove unattended.

## Safety in the Bathroom

Turn on the cold water before turning on the hot water so you don't burn yourself in the bath or shower. Never leave a bathtub or sink full of water and leave the room. This can be dangerous for any younger siblings in your family. No chemical cleaners should be in a place where young children can reach them.

## Electric Safety

Electrical outlets have live electricity in them, so make sure to never stick anything into an outlet. You also want to keep anything that uses batteries or electricity far away from water.

## Fire Safety

The majority of fires start in the kitchen, so it is really important to be extremely careful when cooking. To avoid fires, make sure the oven, stove, toaster, and other appliances are turned off after use. Every home should have a working smoke detector which will make a loud signal if smoke is nearby. A fire extinguisher can be kept in the home to put out small fires. Families should have a plan to get outside as quickly as possible by knowing where all the exits are in the home. Once outside, there should be one central meeting place. Matches and lighters should not be within reach of children and they should never be played with because they are not toys.

## Emergencies

When there is a medical, fire, or other emergency, you can dial 911 from any phone and an emergency operator will send the fire department or police to help you. This number should only be dialed when there is a real emergency. It is important to know your address so they can get to your home easily.

## Internet Safety

There is a new danger today and that is on the internet. If you are ever on a computer or video game, you should never give out any information on a "chat" feature. A lot of video games have an extra part that allows players to connect all over the country and talk to each other. This seems innocent, but there are some people who use this feature to try and get information about you and your family. Always make sure the chat option is turned off and don't communicate with people you don't know.

## Climbing and Playing Safety

Playing or running near the stairs is not a good idea because you could fall down them and get hurt. Climbing a ladder is also dangerous without parental supervision. It's better to climb on any playground equipment you have at your house or at a nearby playground that is built for your age. When you're riding your bicycle or a skateboard, you should wear a helmet to protect your head if you fall.

## Weapons Safety

If there are any guns in your home, make sure you never touch them unless you are with a parent and they are teaching you about proper gun safety and use. Guns should never be used by any children as a toy or for fun. Even if you think a gun is not loaded, you still should never touch it. Ask your parents to put it away in a safe place that is hidden.

We have two projects for your child to choose from. Pick one to complete for the final presentation in this unit, or do both according to your time and resources.

Project 1: Home Safety Check

Project 2: Safety at Home Poster

# Home Safety Checklist

Psalm 4:8 NKJV "I will both lie down in peace, and sleep; for You alone, O Lord, make me dwell in safety."

We never have to live in fear that we are not safe. God has promised to always protect us and keep us safe. He also gives people wisdom and helps them make good decisions. You and your family can ask God to help you to make your home safe for everyone.

Creating a fire escape plan is one of the most important things for every family to have. This is when you practice leaving the house in 2 different ways. If there is a fire in one area, you can all still get outside safely by using a different exit. You will want to practice having a fire drill by walking out calmly and creating a meeting place outside that everyone knows about. You also want to practice "Stop, Drop, and Roll." If anyone is ever wearing clothes that catch on fire, they should stop moving, drop to the ground, and roll. This will help put the fire out.

Today, you will work through a Home Safety Checklist and make sure your home is set up for success in all different categories. You can use the checklist with your family to make sure everyone knows how to stay safe in case of a fire.

Materials Needed:

• Home Safety Checklist page
• Pen or pencil
• Fire extinguisher and carbon monoxide detector

Directions:

First, together with your family, go through the first 3 items in the

Family Training Items section of the Home Safety Checklist. Check off as each item is completed.

Second, with a parent, go through the other safety items in the list and check off as each one is completed:

Is there a fire extinguisher in the kitchen and ready to use? This can put out a small fire in the house more quickly than waiting for the fire department.

Carbon monoxide is a dangerous gas that can make you sick if it is in your home. You cannot smell this gas, but a carbon monoxide detector will beep loudly if carbon monoxide is in your home.

A smoke detector is a sensor that will beep if smoke is nearby. There should be a working detector on every floor of your home.

Matches and lighters should not be within reach of children. They can start a fire.

Cleaning chemicals are also dangerous and should be put away in a safe place.

A parent can check internet filters and video game chats.

Make sure there are no plugged in items like a radio or curling iron near water in the bathroom.

Ask parent to double check that guns are hidden away.

Check that helmets fit and are available for all bike riders.

The number 911 and your home address should be posted in a central location like the kitchen in case of emergency.

Check that there are 1 or 2 working flashlights in the home and extra batteries are available.

Congratulations, you just made your home extra safe!

Save your Home Safety Checklist for your final presentation at the end of this Safety Unit.

# Home Safety Checklist

Family Training Items:

| | |
|---|---|
| Practice stop, drop, and roll | |
| Pick an outside emergency meeting spot | |
| Practice escaping fire in home - 2 exits | |

| | |
|---|---|
| Fire extinguisher is located in kitchen | |
| Carbon monoxide detector in home | |
| Smoke detectors are working | |
| Matches and lighters are hidden | |
| Dangerous chemicals are put away from young children | |
| Have parent check internet filters | |
| No electric or battery items near water in bathrooms | |
| Guns are hidden and locked up | |
| Helmets available for all bike riders | |
| 911 and home address is posted near the phone in case of emergency | |
| Working flashlights with extra batteries | |

# Safety at Home Poster

Psalm 32:7 NKJV "You are my hiding place; You shall preserve me from trouble; You shall surround me with songs of deliverance."

As you read in this week's lesson, there are so many different rules and instructions to remember about how to keep a home safe for everyone. Some of these are memorized eventually, but for now it is helpful to have a poster to help you with all the rules. Today, you will make a poster to hang up in your home to remind you and your family how you can stay safe.

Materials Needed:

- Black marker
- Large construction paper
- Safety at Home information pages
- Glue
- Scissors
- Crayons
- Ruler

Directions:

First, use a ruler to draw a straight line down the center of your construction paper. Use the marker to write DO on the top of one side and DON'T on the top of the other side.

Second, cut out the title of your poster and write your last name in the blank. Glue this to the top middle of your construction paper poster.

Third, cut out the Safety at Home Information pages.

Next, draw a pictures in each rule.

Now, glue each box to the DO or DON'T side of your poster depending on what instruction is in each box.

Save your Safety at Home Poster for your final presentation at the end of this Safety Unit.

# Safety at Home Information

Safety at the _____ Home

Always wear a helmet when riding a bicycle.

**Don't** touch the stove.

**Don't** climb on a ladder without parental supervision.

Pick a central family meeting spot outside your home.

Keep scissors pointed down when carrying them.

# Safety at Home Information

Use an oven mitt to take things out of the oven and keep pot handles aimed away from the front of the stove.

**Don't** touch any guns, knives, matches, or lighters.

Lock doors when you leave home.

Call 911 in an emergency and give them our address:

_____

_____

**Don't** put electric or battery items near water.

# Week 2: Safety Away from Home

**Psalm 62:1** NLT "He alone is my rock and my salvation, my fortress where I will never be shaken."

Being safe away from home is a lot like being safe at home. We depend first on the Lord to keep us safe and trust in His divine protection. He loves you so much and sends angels to surround you and keep you safe. However, there are certain things you can do too. You can learn these simple tips that come from wisdom and safety experts. If you follow all of them, you will keep yourself out of unnecessary danger.

The first rule for safety is to obey your parents. They have rules for you because they want to keep you safe. They love you so much and know some things that you might not know yet. Obeying your mom and dad is a command from God and it brings a blessing back onto you.

**Ephesians 6:1-3** NLT "Obey your parents because you belong to the Lord, for this is the right thing to do. 'Honor your father and mother.' This is the first commandment with a promise. If you honor your father and mother, 'things will go well for you, and you will have a long life on the earth.'"

## Animal Safety

If you see a cute pet you don't know, you might want to run up and touch it. It's smarter to first ask the owner if that would be alright. Some pets might think you are a threat and defend their owner. Also, never grab or pet an animal that is eating.

## Stranger Safety

God loves people, and we love people. We should all pray for people because God loves them so much. His desire is for all people to inherit His kingdom and eternal life. It is important to show love and be kind to all of our friends and family. **Strangers** are people that you don't know. You can see strangers everywhere you go, every day. We know that some people in the world don't know the Lord, and some people are not nice. There are even people who commit crimes and break rules and laws. It is impossible to look at a stranger and know if they are a kind person or a dangerous person. So even though it might seem rude, it is very important to never talk to a stranger. You should never go anywhere with a stranger, even if they are asking for your help. There are lots of ways for a stranger to get help other than you. You should walk away very quickly and tell a police officer or someone else in charge if there is a person trying to ask you personal questions like your name or address. Always tell your mom or dad about anyone who is making you feel uncomfortable or scared in any way.

## Beach and Pool Safety

When you are at the beach or pool with your family, you should always stay close where they can see you. If you are not a strong swimmer, wear a flotation device to help you. Ask your parents if you can get swim lessons. It is a good idea to always have a swim buddy with you. Stick together and don't go anywhere on your own. Make it a habit to wear sunscreen on your face and body when you are out in the sun. Never leave through any gate or fenced in area without talking to your parents first.

## Name and Address Safety

Do you know your full name and address? Do you know the names of your mom and dad? If not, learn them right away. If you ever need help from a police officer or security guard, they will need this important information.

## Store and Playground Safety

When out in a store, at the mall, or on the playground, it is good to have a buddy with you at all times. You should never go anywhere alone, and always stay with your parent. If you notice that you are lost, stay where you are. Make sure to never leave the area and try to find your family on your own. They will be looking for you in the area where you got lost. If you keep moving, it will be harder for your parents to find you. If people stop and want to help you, ask them to call the police or a security guard who will make sure you and your parents are reconnected as quickly as possible. Try to stay calm and patient, and pray to the Lord and ask Him for help.

## Crowd Safety

When you are in a crowd like at a parade, festival, or church event, it is smart to hold hands with someone in your group or your parent. When you first arrive, choose a central location with your parent that will be the meeting place in case you get separated from each other. Also when you first arrive, work together with your parents to identify what the workers are wearing so you can recognize who they are if you need help.

## Police Officers and Security Guards

There are many people who serve the community as security

guards and police officers. They wear uniforms and have a badge to show they are in charge. These are the people you want to talk to if you are ever lost or in an emergency and need help. Their whole job is to help keep the people in your town or city where you live safe. They carry a lot of equipment and even a gun so they might look scary, but you can trust police officers to help you. We should always listen and follow their instructions.

**Titus 3:1** NLT "Remind the believers to submit to the government and its officers. They should be obedient, always ready to do what is good."

We have two projects for your child to choose from. Pick one to complete for the final presentation in this Safety Unit, or do both according to your time and resources.

Project 1: Safety Book

Project 2: Police Officer Project

# Safety Book

**Psalm 4:6-7** NLT "Don't worry about anything; instead, pray about everything. Tell God what you need, and thank Him for all he has done. Then you will experience God's peace, which exceeds anything we can understand. His peace will guard your hearts and minds as you live in Christ Jesus."

There are so many things to remember about what to do and what not to do in different situations when you are away from home. The number one rule to remember is to obey your parents and trust that they know what is best for you. Rules can seem strict, but they are all there to keep you safe. God loves you too and you can absolutely trust in Him. He is faithful. Today, you will make a helpful Safety Book to remember all of the safety rules that are important to know when you are away from home.

## Materials Needed:

- Construction paper
- Scissors
- Color pencils, crayons, and markers
- Glue

## Directions:

**First**, cut out the Safety Book pages. Write your name and date on the cover. Use the information from the lesson to fill in the blanks on each page with a pencil, then a thin marker.

**Second**, use your color pencils and crayons to color in the pictures.

**Third**, put them on top of each other and fold together to make a book. Staple in the middle to keep the book attached together.

**Now**, glue the cover with the date and your name onto the front of the book. Glue one colored page onto each book page. Leave the back cover blank.

Save your Safety Book for your final presentation at the end of this Safety Unit.

# My Safety Book

by

_____
Name

_____
Date

# Stranger Safety

Don't talk to strangers or go anywhere with them even if they ask for _____.

# Crowd Safety

Hold _____ with your parent or friend so you don't get separated. Have a meeting location picked out ahead of time.

# Beach Safety

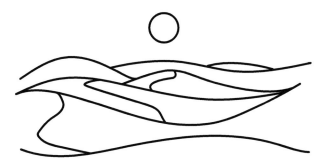

Stay close by your family where they can _____ you and wear a flotation device if you are not a strong _____.

# Animal Safety

Ask the owner before touching their pet. Never touch a pet who is _____.

# Name and Address Safety

Memorize your address and your full name and the full names of your _____ and _____ to tell a police officer if you get lost.

# Playground and Store Safety

If you can't find your parent, don't leave

and search on your own. Stay in the

same _____where you got lost.

# Police Officer Project

Police officers have a very dangerous job. There are some criminals who want to escape and will shoot at officers or try to hurt them. Officers have to keep everyone safe and that includes people who are breaking the rules. We can pray for our police officers to be safe and have wisdom to do their jobs well.

**Matthew 5:9** NKJV "Blessed are the peacemakers, for they shall be called sons of God."

**Luke 11:21** NKJV "When a strong man, fully armed, guards his own palace, his goods are in peace."

## Did You Know?

In the American colonies, before there were police officers, churches had the job of catching criminals and stopping them.

The official name for police is an LEO, Law Enforcement Officer.

Police officers spend most of their time on paperwork, solving cases, and patrolling the community. Only 20% of their time on average is spent chasing or apprehending criminals.

For this project, you will visit a police station and give them a You're Our Heroes note with a yummy treat OR you will make a Police Officer Tools poster.

# You're Our Heroes!
## with a yummy treat

## Materials Needed:

- You're Our Hero page
- Pencil or pen
- Scissors
- Color pencils, crayons and markers
- Ingredients to make a homemade treat
- Disposable food container

## Directions:

**First**, cut out the You're Our Heroes page and fill it out. In the blanks, pick one of the following sentences or mix and match to make up your own:

Thank you for keeping my family and I safe. You are brave! Thank you for serving our community. We appreciate you! Thank you for working hard to help people. You're our heroes!

**Second**, draw a picture in the box at the bottom of the page. You can draw a picture of a police officer, the police station, an officer with his police dog, or a police car. You can even draw a picture of a police officer and you together.

**Third**, bake cookies, bread, or another homemade treat.

Visit the nearby police station and bring your gift of food and the You're Our Heroes note. Get a picture of yourself with a police officer or in front of the station.

Save a picture from your police visit for your final presentation at the end of this Safety Unit.

# You're Our Heroes!

_____

_____

_____

_____

_____

_____

# Police Officers Tools

## Materials Needed:

- Police Officers Tools Information page
- Police Officers with car page
- Police Officers Tools page
- Large sheet of blue construction paper
- Scissors
- Glue
- Color pencils, crayons, and markers

## Directions:

**First**, cut out and color the police officers with car page and glue it down to a piece of construction paper.

**Second**, cut out the Police Officers Tools page and color in each picture. Glue the title Police Officer Tools to the top center of the construction paper.

Read the Police Officer Tools Information page. Use this information to glue the police officer tools onto the construction paper. Draw a line from the tool picture to the police officers page where each one is located.

Save your Police Officer Tools project for your final presentation at the end of this Safety Unit.

# Police Officers Tools Information

**Flashlight**: A lot of crimes happen at night so this tool helps police officers see all the details.

**Gun/Taser**: This weapon is an important tool for self-defense and to stop anyone putting lives in danger.

**Badge**: This tool shows us that this is an official police officer and we need to respect and obey their requests.

**Police car**: Police officers drive these fast cars that can get them to where they need to be quickly and safely. They have special computers and equipment inside and outside.

**Magnifying glass**: Detectives use this tool to look for clues and fingerprints.

**Radio**: This is their essential tool for communicating to other police officers and for getting up to date information. Video footage keeps a record of all the details of their busy days.

**Handcuffs**: This tool keeps criminals confined and in custody.

**Safety vest**: This is made of special material that can protect police from danger.

**Whistle**: This can be used to get the attention of a crowd or help direct traffic.

**Siren and lights**: Police cars have a siren and light on the roof which can warn other cars to get out of the way.

# Police Officers Tools

| | |
|---|---|
| flashlight | radio / video |
| gun / taser | handcuffs |
| badge<br><br>POLICE | safety vest |
| magnifying glass | whistle |
| police car<br><br>POLICE | siren and lights |

# Week 3: Bike and Car Safety

**Psalm 62:2** NKJV "He only is my rock and my salvation; He is my defense; I shall not be greatly moved."

## What is traffic safety?

Our roads are full of cars, trucks, buses, and vans. There are rules we can follow to stay safe near roads and traffic, whether we are in a car or walking near a road.

## Seat Belts

Every single time you are riding in a car, you must wear a seat belt. This can save your life if you are ever in a car accident.

## Windows

Keep your hands and head inside and not hanging out the window to avoid other cars driving near you.

## Horseplay

When you're riding in a vehicle, you don't want to be distracting to the driver. This is not the place to be throwing things, wrestling, or jumping around. Yelling or fighting can also be very distracting for a driver. They need to pay full attention to the road and to other vehicles.

## Doors/Windows

Always double check before closing any doors, windows, or the trunk. Make sure they are clear and nobody is near them. Never play in the trunk of a car.

## Parking Lots

Be extra careful walking in a parking lot, especially behind any vehicles. They might pull out and not be able to see you. Stay with your parent and let them tell you when it is safe to walk.

## Crosswalks

Crosswalks are located at some busy street corners. They have marked lines where all pedestrians should cross the street. If you are crossing at one of these intersections, make sure to stay in the crosswalk. If there is a crossing guard, follow their instructions.

## Traffic Lights

When you have a green light, that is the signal to go. A red light means stop and do not cross. A yellow light means that the green is about to change and the light is about to turn red. Green lights are on the bottom of the traffic light, yellow is in the middle, and red is on the top. When everyone follows the rules of traffic lights, the streets are safe.

## Playing Outside

When you are playing outside near a road or even in front of your home, it is very important to pay attention and always be looking for cars driving by. If you are playing with a ball and it rolls into the street, do not chase it. Stop first and look both ways onto the street to make sure no cars are coming. You can also tell an older sibling or your parents and they can get the ball for you safely. We never play in the street or near railroad tracks.

## Walking/Biking

If you are on a walk or riding a bike or skateboard, the safest place is on the sidewalk. If you must walk near the road, stay on the right side of the road going with the traffic. Stay as close to the curb as you can and out of the way of the vehicles. If you're wearing bright or white clothing, drivers will be able to see you better. Your bike has reflectors on it to make you more visible to drivers and there are clothes with reflectors on them that can keep you safe. Before going outside to play, walk, or bike, double check that your shoes or sneakers are tied and double knot the laces so they don't come untied. You could trip over untied laces.

## Busy roads

There are some roads that you should never walk on. These are busy roads with a lot of traffic or highways. Ask your parents before going on a walk or bike ride and they will tell you which streets are safe for you and which streets you should stay away from.

## Cell phones/Electronics

When we are driving, walking, or biking near a road, it can be distracting to look at a cell phone or other device. If you need to talk to someone or look up directions, it is best to stop what you are doing and focus on that for a minute. Then you can continue on your way. Many accidents and falls happen when people are focused on their electronic devices and not paying attention to what they are doing. For example, instead of trying to record yourself doing a trick on your bike, ask a friend or parent to record you while you focus on riding.

God will always watch over you and keep you safe. We also need to do our part and pay attention to cars and traffic around us. Following these simple rules will keep us safe and allow us to live a long life, serving and loving Jesus, and others.

We have two projects for your child to choose from. Pick one to complete for the final presentation in this Safety Unit, or do both according to your time and resources.

Project 1: Bicycle Safety

Project 2: Traffic Safety Poster

# Bicycle Safety

**Psalm 23:4** NLT "Even when I walk through the darkest valley, I will not be afraid, for you are close beside me. Your rod and your staff protect and comfort me."

Traffic can be dangerous, and that is why we stay out of the street and away from cars. The safest place to walk and ride a bicycle is on the sidewalk. When riding a bike, there are several rules that we want to remember to make sure we are doing everything we can to have a safe ride.

Before riding, you want to check yourself and your bike. It should have tires that are fully inflated. The seat should be about the same height as your handlebars. If you are standing over the bike, the seat should be below you. The seat should be tightened so it does not move while riding. Your helmet should fit snugly and not move around if you shake your head. Wear a bright colored or white shirt and reflectors if possible. Double knot your sneaker or shoelaces so they don't get caught in your bike wheels.

Once you are riding, there are different rules to think about. Stay on the right side of the road and always ride in a single file and not next to another bike. Make a complete stop at all stop signs and red traffic lights. Keep an eye out and watch carefully for any cars driving on the same road and stay out of the way. Before turning or stopping, use your left hand to make a signal while your right hand stays on the handlebars. Put your hand **down** to signal **STOP**. Put you hand to the **left** to signal a **LEFT** turn. Put your hand **up** to signal a **RIGHT** turn. This will allow any cars near you to know what you are doing and stay out of your way.

Today, you will make a checklist that you can keep near your bike to remind you of all the Bicycle Safety rules.

## Materials Needed:

- Construction paper
- Bicycle Safety Checklist page
- Crayons or markers
- Scissors
- Glue
- String or masking tape

## Directions:

**First**, cut out the Bicycle Safety Checklist and color in all of the pictures.

**Second**, glue your Bicycle Safety Checklist to a piece of construction paper.

**Third**, punch holes in the top two corners and tie a string through the holes. Now you can hang your checklist in the garage near your bicycle. Or you can use masking tape to tape your checklist to the wall near where you keep your bike.

Practice riding your bike in the driveway or at the park and use the new hand signals you've learned.

Keep your finished Bicycle Safety Checklist to share in your final presentation at the end of this Safety Unit.

# Bicycle Safety Checklist

☐ Check that the tires are inflated.

☐ Adjust the seat height and make sure it is tightened.

☐ Wear a bright shirt or jacket and reflective gear.

☐ Wear a helmet that fits snugly.

☐ Double check that your shoes are tied well.

☐ Ride on the right side of the road, with the traffic.

☐ Use the correct hand signals when turning.

right    left

☐ Come to a complete stop at stop signs and red lights.

stop

☐ Avoid riding at night.

☐ Ride in single file.

☐ Lock your bike and don't leave it unattended.

# Traffic Safety Poster

**Psalm 37:3** NLT "Trust in the Lord and do good. Then you will live safely in the land and prosper."

Today, you will make a Traffic Safety Poster with many of the rules you learned this week. You can share it with your neighbors and friends and teach them what you know so everyone will be safe. We never have to worry about some bad accident happening, but God does want us to use wisdom and keep ourselves and our younger siblings out of danger. You can teach everything you learned about traffic safety to your family and help watch them when they are outside near the street too.

## Materials Needed:

- Traffic Safety Poster page
- Construction paper
- Color pencils and crayons
- Scissors
- Glue
- Sticky notes

## Directions:

**First**, cut out the boxes on the Traffic Safety Rules page. Fill in the blanks in each sentence and color the pictures.

**Second**, glue the title Traffic Safety on the middle of a construction paper. Glue the other boxes onto the page surrounding the title.

**Third**, write in 2 more rules of your choice from this week on white paper. Draw a picture for each. Glue them onto your Traffic Safety Poster.

Use your Traffic Safety Poster to teach your siblings or friends about safety. Cover over the blanks with sticky notes. Ask them what they think the missing words are.

Lift up the flaps to show them the correct words underneath.

Keep your finished Traffic Safety Poster to share in your final presentation at the end of this Safety Unit.

# Traffic Safety

Wear a _____
while riding in any vehicle.

Don't play in the
_____.

Look both ways before _____
the street.
Use the crosswalk.

Watch out for fingers and
people when closing the car
_____.

## Week 4: Safety Presentation

When we learn about safety, it is so comforting to know that the Lord is the number one way we can be safe. He is always watching over His children because He loves us so much. It is a promise from the Father that He will protect you.

**2 Thessalonians 3:3** NLT "But the Lord is faithful; he will strengthen you and guard you from the evil one."

**Psalm 91:2** NLT "This I declare about the Lord: He alone is my refuge, my place of safety; he is my God, and I trust him."

There is power in our words, and we can memorize and say these scriptures out loud when we find ourselves in a dangerous situation.

Some dangerous situations are easily avoided by the way we live. We can make good choices inside our homes, outside our homes, and on the road. God liberally gives wisdom to those who ask for it, and His wisdom helps us to make smart decisions.

Some good choices are to always obey the rules and our parents. Many rules are set to keep ourselves and those around us safe. Certain items are dangerous and really not for children, such as guns or other weapons and fire.

When away from home, we should always stay with a parent or family member and stay away from strangers. Even if they are asking you for help, it is a good idea to get away and let someone older help them. You can also tell your parents and ask them to help the stranger.

No matter where you are: in a store, at the beach, or on your own street, always stay by your family and don't wander off alone. Picking a meeting spot in advance is so helpful in case your group does get separated.

Police officers are here to help us and keep us safe, and it is smart to have your parents' names and your address memorized so they can help you quickly. Knowing the numbers 911 is also important because we can dial that on any phone to get immediate help.

When playing outside near a road, we should always be aware of cars and traffic. It is easier for you to see a car than it is for someone in a car to see you. Whether we are riding in a car, or we are outside walking near cars, staying vigilant and aware of what is going on around you will keep you safe. Electronics are fun but should only be used when you are not near traffic.

These are a lot of rules to memorize about how to stay safe, but they will come naturally the more you practice them. You can ask God to keep you safe and healthy as you start your day, and we can trust in His safety net around us when we make a mistake. He is always faithful.

This unit's presentation will remind you of all the many ways to stay safe no matter where you are or what you are doing. Sharing it with those you love this week will probably remind them of some safe behaviors that they may have been forgetting to do. But you can also remind them that the only way we can stay 100% perfectly safe is to stay in the presence of God.

# Preparing Your Presentation

## Materials Needed:

- Trifold or poster board
- Scissors
- Tape/glue
- Pen/pencils
- Crayons/markers
- Pictures and projects from the previous weeks
- Construction paper

## Directions:

Make a trifold or poster board of all your observations about Safety from the three previous weeks. Include pictures you took of your projects and the projects you made. You can use the trifold diagram below as an example, but your board is yours to make your own; be creative and have fun. Make sure to include the unit title and the driving question. Then invite a relative or family friend over to present what you found out about safety. Use the checklists on the following pages as a guide to prepare for your presentation.

**Psalm 91:2** NLT "This I declare about the Lord: He alone is my refuge, my place of safety; he is my God, and I trust him."

**Psalm 62:1** NLT "He alone is my rock and my salvation, my fortress where I will never be shaken."

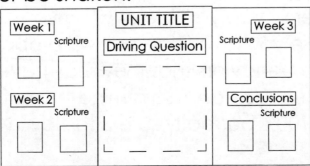

# Unit 6
# Trifold/Board Checklist

I have the UNIT TITLE on my trifold/board.

| **Safety** |
|---|

I have the driving question on my trifold/board.

| **How can I live safely?** |
|---|

I use pictures, drawings, and props on my trifold/board.

I practice how I am going to use my trifold/board.

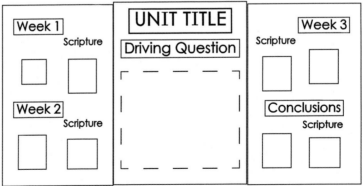

I did my best job on my trifold/board.

# Unit 6
# Presentation Checklist

I plan what I am going to say for my presentation.

I practice speaking loud and clear for my presentation.

I look at my audience during my presentation.

I answer questions from the audience after my presentation.

I will do my best on the presentation.